The Good Dog Library

Best Behavior

Unleashing Your Dog's Instinct to Obey

ISBN: 1-879-620-65-0

Please note: The information appearing in this publication is presented for educational purposes only. In no case shall the publishers or authors be held responsible for any use readers may choose to make, or not to make, of this information.

Belvoir Publications Inc.
Box 2626
75 Holly Hill Lane
Greenwich, CT 06836 USA

Best Behavior Unleashing Your Dog's Instinct to Obey
The editors of Your Dog and Whole Dog Journal

ISBN: 1-879-620-65-0
1. Dogs-Behavior   2. Canine   3. Canine Behavior

Manufactured in the United States of America

The Good Dog Library

Best Behavior

Unleashing Your Dog's Instinct to Obey

Edited by Diane L. Muhlfeld

Belvoir Publications, Inc.
Greenwich, CT

Contents

Section III: Early Learning

Section IV: Behavior Problems and Solutions

Preface

They sit and watch, eager to please and to play, waiting for the slightest hint of acknowledgement or recognition from the owners they love. Unable to speak their minds, dogs communicate with a look, a whimper, a bark, a swish of a tail. And while these signs may be subtle and elusive, they nonetheless are the manifestation of your dog's personality. And what a personality it is!

Your dog may not be able to show it, but he thinks and laughs and sheds real tears—indeed, feels the full range of emotions from joy to sorrow to fear to desire, just as we do. It's our job as owners—and our privilege, too—to understand our dogs' fascinating dimensions and to respond appropriately to their many needs, both physical and emotional.

Best Behavior, the first book in THE GOOD DOG LIBRARY, offers insight, instruction, and sheds new light on what your family pet is all about—how dogs' primordial instincts still govern their modern actions, how they communicate amongst themselves and with us, and the many developmental stages they pass through as they progress from playful pup to old and trusted friend.

You will learn how to integrate that new dog into your family's life, how "the pack" forms the nexus of their world, how your dog learns and grows, and lastly, how behavior problems—from separation anxiety to inappropriate chewing—can be understood and overcome.

Throughout *Best Behavior*, professional trainers, behaviorists and veterinarians offer current theories and practical solutions—both traditional and alternative—to everyday interactions with our beloved canine pals—enabling us to give our special animal friends the single greatest gift we can give—a welcome role as a true member of the family.

Subsequent volumes in THE GOOD DOG LIBRARY will address common medical conditions and treatments; training in the early years and beyond; nutrition, care and grooming; the intricacies of breeds and personalities; canine physiology and anatomy, and illuminating case histories.

We hope you'll join us as we begin our journey with our canine companions.

Diane L. Muhlfeld
Greenwich, Connecticut
March 2000

Section I

The Essential Dog

1

Your Dog's Lifespan

In general, small dogs live longer than large dogs, and small-breed puppies mature faster than large-breed puppies.

The phrase "a dog's age" suggests a long period of time. In truth, however, our canine companions don't usually live as long as our human loved ones. But the better you understand your dog's aging "schedule," the better you'll be at detecting—and perhaps preventing—certain age-related behavioral and medical problems.

The Aging Enigma

Aging is a complex biological process governed by genetic "programming" and environmental factors such as nutrition. Aging results in a progressive reduction in an animal's ability to withstand stress and disease. Most of what veterinarians believe about the physiology of canine aging is extrapolated from studies on people and laboratory animals. "Of all the physiological phenomena we study, aging is among the most mysterious," concedes Dr. Larry Engelking, professor of physiology at Tufts University School of Veterinary Medicine.

If the aging process in dogs is similar to that in people, an aging dog's basal metabolic rate (energy consumption at rest) slows, the amount of lean muscle and water in its body decreases, and the relative proportion of fat increases—even if the dog's body weight remains constant.

In people (and, we suspect, in dogs), aging is also accompanied by a gradual but inexorable loss of organ function. The number of liver and nervous-system cells decreases, lungs lose their elasticity, the kidneys become less able to filter wastes, the volume of blood pumped by the heart decreases, and the immune system's ability to fight off infection declines.

Lifespan Variability

Aging dogs display several observable characteristics. Their activity level drops (which owners of hyperactive pooches may find a blessing), and many dogs' muzzles turn white with age, the result of atrophied hair-pigment cells. But when these signs of aging appear varies widely from dog to dog.

In general, small dogs live longer than large dogs, although no one knows exactly why, and small-breed puppies mature faster than large-breed puppies. Thus, a pint-sized pug is likely to be physically "grown up" by 9 to 12 months of age, while a giant Newfoundland may continue growing until it's 2 or 3 years old. When aging factors including size are equalized, neutered dogs tend to live longer than their intact counterparts—perhaps because the stay-at-home tendencies of neutered pets keep them out of harm's way.

■ Busy Young'uns

Rapid-fire physical and behavioral changes occur during the first 12 to 24 months of a dog's life. Especially during their first 4 to 6 months, puppies learn very quickly. "Owners who socialize and train a dog to behave appropriately at this stage are likely to encounter fewer behavior problems later," notes Dr. Gerry Flannigan, a resident at the Behavior Clinic at Tufts University School of Veterinary Medicine.

■ The "Teenage Years"

Dogs become sexually mature—usually at about 6 to 9 months old—well before they become behaviorally mature—which for some dogs takes up to 3 years. Thus, no matter how well-trained and socialized, an adolescent dog (from 4 or 6 months to 12 or 18 months of age) can be a challenge to live with.

Some animal behaviorists liken this stage to a human's teenage years, complete with the testing of preestablished boundaries. It's therefore important to maintain firm but humane leadership and to continue to reinforce training during this time.

■ The Plateau of Adulthood

If a dog has received adequate health care, consistent training, and ample socialization, adulthood is usually a relatively uneventful period. Nevertheless, during this life stage some late-onset genetic diseases (such as progressive retinal atrophy) and behavioral problems (such as noise phobias) may crop up.

■ Golden Oldies

Although aging itself is not a disease, the golden years may bring diseases uncommon in younger dogs. These include diabetes mellitus; kidney, heart, and liver disease; hormonal anomalies such as Cushing's disease; arthritis; periodontal disease; and cancer. Owners of older dogs should look out for any signs of pain, changes in body weight, variations in ingestion or elimination habits such as increased water intake and urine output, joint stiffness, skin and mouth growths, and decreased interaction with people and the environment. To catch age-related disorders at the earliest possible stage, veterinarians often perform disease-screening blood tests during annual checkups for older dogs.

Ages and Stages

The first 12 to 24 months of a dog's life are comparable to human infancy, childhood, adolescence, and young adulthood.

The adult stage in dogs (from age 2 or 3 to 7 or 8, assuming a 12-year lifespan) is approximately comparable to the human ages of 25 through 50.

The point at which a dog qualifies as "aged" varies. Veterinarians generally consider small dogs to be senior citizens at about 12 years of age, while large dogs reach the senior stage at 6 to 8 years of age. This roughly corresponds to the 55-plus category in people.

Time Stops for No Dog

No one has discovered the canine "fountain of youth," but there are things you can do to stall the sands of time. Nutrition is key. Nutritionally speaking, there are only two "official" canine life stages. One is adult maintenance, and the other is growth and reproduction (which includes growing puppies and pregnant and nursing mothers). Pet-food companies have created an unofficial, arbitrary "senior" life stage for dogs, but "we don't know for certain what older dogs as a group need nutritionally," says Dr. Lisa Freeman, assistant professor and nutritionist at Tufts University School of Veterinary Medicine. "So there's no reason to automatically switch a healthy 7- or 8-year-old dog to a so-called 'senior' diet."

Research in people has shown that obesity decreases life expectancy. While this may be true in dogs, no one has proven it. In fact, some older dogs lose rather than gain weight. "When it comes to nutrition, treating older dogs as individuals is extremely important," Dr. Freeman emphasizes.

Appropriate levels of exercise are also critical. "The phrase 'use it or lose it' is especially applicable to older dogs," notes Dr. Engelking. And while canine seniors may not be the intellectual sponges their younger cohorts are, "if you keep an older dog mentally stimulated as well as physically active, you'll improve its quality of life," says Dr. Flannigan.

Perhaps your best hedge against your dog growing old before its time is the annual checkup. Remember, a yearly exam for a dog is roughly equivalent to your seeing a physician every 5 years. So don't overlook those routine veterinary visits. ❖

2

The New Puppy

Your behavior during the first year—especially those first few months—can mean the difference between a well-adjusted companion and a canine calamity.

F ew things bring as much joy—or as much responsibility— as the arrival of a new family member (be it two-legged or four-legged). When the newcomer is a puppy, each day yields discovery and adventure. What happens (or doesn't happen) during your puppy's formative first year—especially during its first 3 months—determines, in large part, whether your dog will grow up to be a well-adjusted family member and good canine citizen. But even if your new companion is an adult dog, understanding how puppyhood experiences shaped its present character can help you and your dog live together in harmony.

Behaviorists categorize the four preadult stages of a dog's life as neonatal (newborn), transitional, socialization, and juvenile. Instead of memorizing when these stages begin and end, it is more impor-

tant that you understand that a puppy is sensitive to outside influences—both canine and human—during each of these stages.

Puppy Tests

*When choosing a puppy, prospective owners often seek
out a specific personality. To assist owners in the selection process, breeders frequently "temperament test" their
puppies at 7 or 8 weeks of age. While techniques vary
somewhat, most puppy tests measure a youngster's will-
ingness to approach and follow a stranger (usually the
tester), as well as the puppy's reactions to sudden noises,
petting, and being picked up and turned over on its back.*

*However, "The jury is still out regarding the predictive
value of puppy temperament tests given at 7 weeks," says
Dr. Dodman, director of the Behavior Clinic at Tufts
University School of Veterinary Medicine. Experts observe
that a puppy that is outgoing at 7 weeks may be shy at 12
weeks. And one that struggles when held on its back (an
ostensible sign of dominance) may grow up to be submissive. One study followed the lives of several hundred
puppies initially tested at 6 to 8 weeks of age, then retest-
ed at 16 weeks, 26 weeks, and 18 months. Many of the
dogs that showed an early attraction to people eventually
became aloof and independent.*

*Because the personalities of dogs are still quite "plastic"
beyond the 7- or 8-week point, early puppy tests are really only useful in predicting extremes of behavior—such
as excessive shyness or dominance. (For example, a 7-
week-old puppy that growls menacingly at a tester usually continues to display aggressive behavior later in life.)
Dr. Dodman suggests that a series of temperament tests—
conducted every 2 weeks from 8 to 14 weeks—may more
accurately predict adult behavior.*

The First Two Weeks

For the first 2 weeks, newborn pups (neonates) simply sleep (often
in a communal heap) and nurse. With unopened eyes and ear canals,

newborns are essentially blind and deaf. Their mobility is limited to sliding on their chests with paddling arms and legs. Smell and touch, however, are operational at this early stage. Scientists believe these senses fire up first to help puppies maintain contact with their mother—their sole source of nourishment.

Much of the neonate's nervous system lacks myelin. (Fatty sheaths of myelin insulate nerves, helping them effectively transmit signals.) Hence, many of the puppy's earliest behaviors are purely reflexive—simple "knee jerk" reactions to outside stimuli. In fact, neonates can't even urinate or defecate unless their mother (or a surrogate) initiates a reflex by stimulating their anal and genital regions.

Reversing the traditional "hands off" policy, many behaviorists now encourage limited human handling of newborn puppies. "There's ample scientific evidence that carefully handling animals from the time they're born significantly accelerates their nervous-system development," says Dr. Nicholas Dodman, director of the Behavior Clinic at Tufts University School of Veterinary Medicine. Studies suggest early human handling may help puppies become better problem solvers, more self-confident in competitive situations with other dogs, and more attracted to people. So, if you're gentle and limit handling to about 10 minutes a day (and, of course, if mom doesn't object), it's virtually never too early to pet a puppy. (Remember: adults should always supervise children handling puppies.)

Transitional Period

Dramatic changes occur during the week known as the transitional period. The puppy's eyelids and ear canals open, and it experiences a barrage of sounds and sights. But puppy vision remains fuzzy until the optic nerve, which carries signals from the eyes to the brain, becomes fully developed during the fourth week.

By the end of the transitional stage, puppies have figured out how to stand and walk, and they often waddle together in a "puppy pack." Playful biting and pawing harbingers what many experts consider the most important stage of a dog's life—the socialization period.

Early Socialization

During the first 3 or 4 weeks of the socialization period (which typically lasts from the third to the twelfth or fourteenth week), the pups' sensory and motor abilities improve at lightning speed, and their repertoire of behaviors expands accordingly. Much to their delight, puppies discover that they can run, and they start communicating vocally and with body postures. Having gained control over their bladders and bowels as well as their limbs, the pups begin to leave the nest to "do their business."

Now more interested in each other than in mom, the puppies engage in riotous play—an entertaining mishmash of biting, chasing, stalking, and wrestling. Play is critically important to a dog's physical and behavioral development. Says Dr. Dodman, "Playing helps puppies learn what does and doesn't offend others, how to say 'I'm sorry,' and how to assert themselves to get what they want." For example, pups learn how hard they can bite before causing their littermates to yip in pain. Considering the razor sharpness of a pup's milk teeth, we should be grateful that socialized pups learn "bite inhibition" from one another.

Puppies deprived of play—for example, those removed from the litter at 4 or 5 weeks of age—often become inappropriately aggressive or fearful around other dogs. And although interactions with littermates take center stage from the third to the seventh week, studies also show that puppies totally deprived of human contact during that time tend to withdraw from people. On the other hand, some young dogs disadvantaged by lack of early human contact are so insecure that once they become attached to a kind owner, they experience separation anxiety when left by themselves.

Fearful Puppies

Puppies between 3 and 5 weeks of age fearlessly explore their environment. But at about 5 weeks, fear of the unfamiliar (including people if the pup hasn't been around them) sets in, putting a damper on puppy pioneering.

Studies point to yet another fearful period—at around 8 weeks of age. Traumatic experiences that occur at this time may become permanently etched in a pup's mind. Eight weeks is also when many people bring puppies into their homes, so "quality time" with the new arrival is all the more essential.

Puppy vaccinations also come due at around 8 weeks of age. Many veterinarians give puppies shots with ultrathin needles and room-temperature vaccines so they don't develop a permanent aversion to animal clinics. Another tip: when the veterinarian gives a vaccination, try offering your puppy a treat to divert the little one from noticing the pinch of the needle. (The same type of distraction may also work for a fearful older dog.)

The Homecoming

By 7 or 8 weeks, puppies exhibit most elements of adult-dog behavior (albeit in comically uncoordinated ways). Many veterinarians and behaviorists believe this is the minimum age at which you should introduce a puppy into a new home. Doing so earlier to meet a personal deadline—such as a relative's birthday—is ill-advised.

Although a puppy makes tremendous strides over the first 7 weeks, it still has a lot to learn about living with humans and other dogs. If you do not immediately begin teaching your pup appropriate dog behavior, it will learn other (often objectionable) behaviors on its own. Therefore, experts encourage as much human guidance as possible during the seventh to fourteenth weeks. Animal behaviorist Ian Dunbar advocates "puppy parties"—informal gatherings where a diverse group of your friends visits and interacts with your puppy. In this way, a puppy learns to associate human handling with "good times."

It's also important to continue socializing your pup with other dogs during weeks 7 to 14. But make sure all animals your dog interacts with are completely immunized. Even if your pup receives all its "puppy shots" on schedule, it won't be completely protected until it's about 16 weeks old.

Many experts consider the socialization period the critical period of development, but it is not a make-or-break situation. Puppies that are minimally exposed to people and other dogs during their first 3 months can—and often do—turn into great family companions. But they must be matched with patient owners are willing to spend time teaching them social skills that most dogs learn at a younger age.

Puppy Potty Training

When housetraining a young puppy (2 to 4 months), there are a number of steps you can take to prevent indoor "accidents":

■ Always take the pup outside just after it wakes from a nap, within 15 minutes after it eats, after "playtime," and immediately if it starts circling and sniffing—a sure sign that something is about to happen, probably momentarily.

■ Determine how long your pup can "hold it." For a pup 4 months old or younger, add 1 to its age in months to get a ballpark estimate of the number of hours it will have bladder/bowel control.

■ Don't let an untrained, unsupervised puppy loose in the house. When you can't supervise your puppy indoors, confine it in a warm, comfortable crate.

■ Neutralize odors at all indoor accident sites. (Ask your veterinarian for advice on which odor busters to use, but avoid ammonia; its urinelike smell is a "pee here" signal to your pup.)

■ If your puppy "slips," do not physically punish it—even if you catch it in the act. This may make it become afraid to "go" outside in your presence.

Juvenile Period

The juvenile period lasts from about 3 months to the time of sexual maturity—anywhere from 6 months to a year. (But, as owners of "perpetual puppies" discover, social maturity may not develop until much later.) During the juvenile period, the dog further refines its motor and social skills. Despite increasing maturity, however, juvenile dogs learn less quickly than their younger counterparts; therefore, training an adolescent dog requires extra time and patience.

While many dogs retain puppy playfulness and the ability to "learn new tricks" throughout their lives, older dogs are not as behaviorally pliant as their younger counterparts. If you're blessed with the opportunity to guide a dog from puppyhood to adulthood, make the most of those early days when nearly everything makes a lasting impression. Your behavior during the first year—especially those first few months—will help shape your dog's future behavior and can mean the difference between a well-adjusted companion and a canine calamity. If you get an older dog instead of a puppy, be prepared to devote extra time and patience to establishing your relationship and developing your mature companion's social skills.

Many of the behavioral changes that occur during the juvenile period are hormone driven—especially in male dogs. The release of testosterone in unneutered males sets off increased roaming, urine-marking, and mounting behavior. In females, hormones trigger estrus (heat), but females show relatively few hormone-mediated behavioral changes.

Vive la Difference

It's a fact of life: boy dogs behave differently than girl dogs. If you understand the differences, you'll better understand your pooch's conduct. This knowledge may also steer you toward one gender over the other if you're planning to adopt a dog.

■ Hormones at the Helm

While a dog's experiences have a significant impact on its behavior, its sex hormones, which start flowing at puberty (between 5 and 6 months of age for males and between 6 and 18 months of age for females), drive many of the pooch's impulses. The pubescent period starts when the youngster's pituitary gland—located at the base of the brain—sends a chemical signal to the gonads (sex glands), stimulating the release of hormones.

An adult male dog with intact testes has a continuous supply of the male hormone testosterone circulating through its body and influencing its behavior. Testosterone stimulates the male to roam in search of a mate, mark its territory with urine, mount objects, and act aggressively. Testosterone also reduces levels of the brain chemical serotonin. "And low levels of serotonin are usually associated with aggression," says Dr. Dodman.

Unlike her male counterpart, the adult female dog with intact ovaries comes under the behavioral influence of sex hormones only a couple of times a year when her ovaries secrete estrogen during heat (estrus) and progesterone during the 60-day period following ovulation (the release of an egg from the ovaries). Estrogen makes the female receptive to male advances, roam to search out a suitor, vocalize frequently, and sometimes, become aggressive. Progesterone, on the other hand, has a calming, almost anesthetic effect on a pooch. However, progesterone can cause some females to "think" they are pregnant—a condition known as pseudopregnancy. During pseudopregnancy, progesterone stimulates the unbred female to show maternal behavior, complete with mammary-gland engorgement.

■ The Makings of a Male

Although behavioral differences between the sexes are most obvious after puberty, prepubescent male pups do display some sex-specific behaviors. "Toward the end of gestation, there is a little burst of testosterone that masculinizes the male pup's brain," says Dr. Dodman. (Female pups have no testosterone surge, so their brains remain "feminine.") Testosterone-induced physical changes in the male fetal brain cause young male pups to take on some of the behaviors of adult males—such as playful mounting of littermates—well before they've experienced the surge of male hormones at puberty. These prenatal changes in brain architecture set the stage for puberty, when the youngster will develop a complete repertoire of male sexual behavior.

■ Altered Behavior

Since many sex-related behaviors are bothersome to owners (and put a roaming dog at risk of parenthood or physical injury), veterinarians typically recommend surgical removal of a dog's gonads—spaying for females and castration for males. The procedure won't change the essential "maleness" or "femaleness" of the dog's brain, so the animal may continue to display some sex-related behaviors. But removing the sex-hormone source is effective in reducing or eliminating many sex-related problem behaviors.

Neutering is most effective at decreasing roaming behavior—with about a 95 percent effectiveness rate. The effect of neutering on aggressive behavior, however, is less clear cut—particularly in females. If a female is aggressive only during heat, spaying should reduce her aggression because she no longer comes into heat. But if she shows aggressive behavior when she's not in heat, spaying may increase her aggression because she will no longer be under the calming influence of progesterone for part of the year. If your intact female is aggressive, talk to your veterinarian about behavior modification (perhaps supplemented by pharmacological therapy) after spaying.

In male dogs, neutering reduces intermale dominance aggression in 60 percent of cases. Testosterone feeds the fire of aggression; without it, the flames subside. Castration also changes a male dog's odor so it's less likely to provoke other males. Postneutering behavior-modification therapy may also dampen any smoldering embers of aggression.

Spaying or neutering a dog early in its life can head off some sex-related behaviors before they become problem behaviors. But even if you have an intact older dog, it's not too late to spay or neuter it. At any age, the surgery is likely to reduce unwanted sex-related behaviors—and it will ensure that your dog isn't contributing to the numbers of unwanted pups. ❧

3

Coming Home

Whether yours is an "only dog" or multi-dog household, your new dog will need peace and quiet when it first comes home.

If you've ever had the privilege of living with a dog, you will, at some time, probably get another one. You'll research the options and select the most appropriate dog—considering age, gender, breed (or mix), and individual temperament. (And, of course, you'll wait until after the holidays so your newcomer doesn't have to cope with that hectic time of year.) You'll also need a plan for the big event itself—your new dog's homecoming.

Prearrival Preparations

Whether your new family member is entering a home with other pets or is destined to enjoy "only dog" status, it's bound to feel more comfortable in an atmosphere of peace and quiet— at least initially. To ensure that, have all the necessary equipment on hand before you pick up your new dog and bring him home: food and water bowls, safe dog toys, warm bedding, collar, leash, identification tags, and grooming supplies. That way, you can spend quiet time helping your new pal adjust to his new life.

Next, "puppy proof" your house—even if your new charge is a mature dog, the excitement of homecoming can trigger mishaps. Remove all shoes, children's toys, and other canine curiosities from the floors; store chemicals out of harm's way; and find new homes for low-lying knickknacks.

In addition to working out homecoming logistics, you need to mentally prepare yourself and your family. If you have youngsters, explain to them that homecoming day may be less joyful for Bowser than it is for them. Teach your children how to pet a dog (gentle strokes—not staccato patting or ear and tail tugging) and encourage them to express excitement in ways other than jumping and shouting when the new dog arrives.

Also, have a schedule in place for your newcomer before arrival. And make sure all family members buy into it. "Dogs, in general, feel more stable and composed with routine schedules of feeding and exercise," says Dr. Nicholas Dodman, director of the Behavior Clinic at Tufts University School of Veterinary Medicine. "Erratic schedules can be stressful to them."

The Young Pup

A low-key transition is especially important when the newcomer is a puppy. Homecoming usually means a traumatic rift in the strong bonds the pup has formed with mother and littermates. To ease your puppy's adjustment, pick it up as early in the day as possible (preferably at the beginning of a weekend or vacation) so you have plenty of time to spend with it.

Puppies often begin to show distress during the car ride home. Arrange to have someone else drive so you can ease your pup's discomfort. Place it in a small crate on your lap or (if the pup is not a "wiggle worm") cradle it in your arms. If you can, bring along an item carrying the scent of the pup's littermates. "The puppy will appreciate some familiar smells during the ride home," suggests Dr. Dodman.

After arriving home, take the pup to its designated "potty" area and lavishly praise it when it does its business. Then take the pup inside to the area that will be its primary home for the first couple of months while it learns "the ropes." The pup should find its bedding, food and water dishes, and toys ready and waiting. Let the pup explore its new abode free from any loud or otherwise scary stimuli. When introducing the pup to children, emphasize that they should be quiet and calm. "Supervised interactions with children will help the puppy associate children with pleasant things," says Dr. Dodman.

The first few nights can be very unsettling for a puppy. Invariably, puppies whimper, whine—even howl heartbreakingly. As hard as it is to ignore these despondent cries, resist the temptation to intervene. The pup almost certainly will cry itself to sleep—unless you reward its vocalizations with extra attention. And scolding a crying pup will only make matters worse.

If you crate your pup at night, place the crate in your bedroom so the pup is comforted by having you nearby. Consider placing a warm hot-water bottle wrapped in a blanket or a softly ticking clock in the crate to simulate litter life and reduce your pup's anxiety. Remember, a pup's initial experiences in and around its new home will make a lasting impression

Crate Training

Because dogs instinctively gravitate to sheltered den-like spaces, a comfortable, appropriately sized crate (large enough for an adult dog to stand and turn around in) can be an important aid in helping your dog acclimate. Crates can also help in housetraining."For most dogs, small spaces are secure spaces," says Dr. Dodman.

But thrusting a dog into a crate and locking the door is a sure way—from a dog's point of view—to turn a potential den into a dungeon. Let the dog go in and out of the crate of its own accord, and don't close the door until the dog seems comfortable inside. "Dens don't have doors," notes Dr. Dodman. Help your dog associate the crate with pleasant experiences by putting treats, meals, water, and toys in the open crate. Never use the crate as punishment.

Once the crate feels like home to your dog, close the crate door and leave the room for gradually increasing periods of time. Don't let the dog out in response to its plaintive vocalization; wait until the dog is quiet before opening the crate door so you reinforce calm behavior.

If you've adopted a dog that shows signs of separation anxiety be careful about introducing a crate. If your dog overreacts at the mere sight of a crate, it's likely that past

experience has taught the dog to associate crates with pun-ishment, and you should therefore not use one. On the other hand, crating can help some dogs with milder forms of separation anxiety feel more secure when left alone.

The Mature Dog

As with puppies, do whatever it takes to make your older dog's homecoming as stress-free as possible. If your new dog is self-confident, you can expect a minimum of fear and insecurity. But if you have a nervous older dog, you may have to do exactly as you would with a puppy.

With the new dog on a leash, show it the "bathroom" outside and its "bedroom" inside; then give it a guided tour of the indoor areas where it will be allowed to go. Offering praise and food treats will make the new sights, sounds, and smells less stressful.

You may want to restrict even an older newcomer to certain areas of the house until it becomes familiar with the surroundings. In fact, don't give any new dog—pup or adult—immediate run of the house and yard. Assign your dog to certain areas for sleeping, eating, and elimination—gradually increasing the boundaries over time. "Confinement is a good way to establish structure," says Brian Kilcommons, noted dog trainer and author of *Good Owners, Great Dogs.*

The Multi-dog Household

Those who love having one dog in the family often introduce a second one later. And every owner's fantasy is that their two dogs will become best buddies. But even if they don't, a properly managed introduction can lay the foundation for peaceful coexistence.

If possible, don't commit to taking a new dog until a trial meeting indicates that the prospective newcomer will interact peacefully with your other dog. (According to Mr. Kilcommons, you'll have a better chance at canine harmony if the new dog is not genetically predisposed to fighting and is the opposite sex of your other dog.) Introduce the prospective housemates in neutral territory (such as a public park) with both on leash. Keep an eye on their interaction, but don't force them together. Let them gather information through sniffing and circling rituals. Separate them if serious snapping breaks out.

If you can't arrange a trial snout-to-snout meeting, consider a "scent exchange" program. Rub a towel over your present pet and bring the towel to the prospective new dog for olfactory analysis. Rub another towel over the new dog, then let dog "number one" smell that towel before introducing the newcomer.

If the preliminaries go well and you decide to bring the new dog home, separately feed and bed the two dogs until they become comfortable with one another. While it is important to keep an eye out for signs of aggression—lip curling, growling, and snapping—remember that dogs prefer hierarchy to democracy and may tussle to establish who's boss. (If the two animals can't live in the same home without continuing violence, however, consider an alternative placement for the second dog. Remember also that an initially chummy relationship may change as the dogs pass through different life stages.)

Avoid your natural tendency to fuss over the newcomer at the expense of your other dog. Conversely, while it may not hurt to initially treat the incumbent as top dog, step back and let the dogs work out the dominance hierarchy. Depending on their respective ages, sizes, genders, and temperaments, either the newcomer or incumbent may eventually emerge as top dog. Once you see which dog has achieved dominance, support that dog's status to avoid confusing both dogs. Meanwhile, maintain your position as the ultimate pack leader and provide each dog with plenty of "quality" time for play, exercise, and grooming.

Fido Meets Felix

If you're thinking of surprising kitty with a canine friend, remember that many cats go undercover when strangers of any species appear. "Under these circumstances, the cat is usually more stressed out than the dog," says Dr. Dodman. You can try the trial-meeting or scent-exchange techniques, but don't be surprised if your cat disappears for a couple of days when Fido enters the domain.

When seeking canine-feline détente, you must have patience. Confine the new dog to one room or area and let the cat approach gradually—on its own terms. For the incumbent cat's sake, make sure Fido doesn't have uncontrollable predatory instincts before you commit to taking the dog. (A puppy is more likely than an older dog to respect a cat as a pack member rather than pursue it as prey.)

Bottom Line

To sum up: When considering adding a four-footed family member, plan carefully. Establish a routine for the new animal in advance and stick to it. Carefully manage the dog's early interactions with other family members so all associations are as positive as possible. Most important, balance your time so all your animal companions get a generous amount of your loving care and attention. ❖

4

Children and Dogs

*The effort you invest in choosing a dog
and carefully introducing it to your children
will pay years of rewards.*

Most adults who had the good fortune to be raised with a dog have fond memories of their childhood companion. When people who were "raised by dogs" (or wish they were) become parents, they naturally want their children to have a joyful, forgiving, never-critical canine pal. Dogs and children are natural allies. In a busy household, where adults may sometimes be preoccupied with work, bills, and household chores, dogs and children concentrate on things that really matter—like exploring and having fun.

But when dogs and children live under the same roof, you must establish some ground rules. Before you come home with a new dog, make sure all family members understand their respective roles in helping the dog learn the rules of its new home. And if you are about to bring a new baby into your dog's world, prepare your dog for the new arrival.

Is a Dog Right for You?

Before you decide *which* dog is right for your family, ask yourself if a dog is *right* for your family. If you have infants or toddlers, you may already have enough demands on your attention. Although most dogs are tolerant of small children, you should never leave a young child alone with any dog—not even a trusted family pet. When a 2-year-old child uses a passing tail or dangling ear as a convenient handle to prevent a fall, your dog may be startled or hurt. Dogs use a vocabulary of postures, facial expressions, growls, and—yes—nips to warn other dogs that they are angry or fearful. Young children can easily misread such warning signals—perhaps mistaking a dog's fearful retreat for a fun game of chase. If you have very young children and do not already have a dog, you might consider postponing getting one until your children are at least 4 or 5 years old.

A Dog for the Whole Family

Sharing in the care of a dog teaches a child responsibility and compassion. And when a child trains a dog to perform a simple trick like "roll over," both the child and the dog learn that persistent effort brings rewards. But proper care of a dog requires the careful supervision of an adult and the cooperation of the entire household.

Before you set out to find a dog, ask yourself how you will allocate responsibilities. Who will walk the dog, feed it, train it, take it to the veterinarian? The allocation of dog-care responsibilities will depend on your children's ages and temperaments, the number of adult family members, work and school schedules, the availability of dog walkers, and many other variables.

Selecting a Dog

Your first consideration in selecting a dog is choosing a breed that is reputed to be good with children and will adapt to your surroundings and lifestyle. There are many helpful books that describe the characteristics of the various dog breeds, but don't rely on books alone. Breed can be an indicator of behavior, but it is not a guarantee. The physical and behavioral characteristics of dogs vary from breeder to breeder. A dog of any breed may have a calm disposition—or, conversely, it could be unusually aggressive or fearful.

Regardless of the dog breed you favor, select a dog with a friendly, tolerant temperament.

Don't overlook mixed-breed dogs when looking for a family pet. They are often intelligent, healthy, and good natured, although it may be difficult to predict the future appearance of a mixed-breed puppy if you don't know its heritage. If you plan to select a mixed-breed dog—puppy or adult—from a shelter, ask the shelter staff to help you select a dog with a temperament that is suitable for a home with children.

Be sure to have your new dog neutered to prevent unwanted puppies and make it a safer pet. A neutered male dog is far less likely to bite than an unneutered (intact) male. And because a spayed female will not come into heat (estrus), she will not attract the unwanted attentions of intact male dogs when you are walking her.

"THE DOG WAS CREATED ESPECIALLY FOR CHILDREN. HE IS THE GOD OF FROLIC."

HENRY WARD BEECHER

Your Dog's New Home

The arrival of your new dog is an exciting time for you and your children, but it can also be a stressful time for the dog. Before you bring the dog home, prepare a sanctuary—ideally, a training crate or dog bed. Remind your children that the dog will need some quiet time as well as play time. You need to teach your children to treat the dog with care and respect at the same time you are teaching your dog the rules of its new home.

Begin a training program at once. Your dog will want to know how to behave in its new "pack." Although an adult family member must take charge of the training, other family members should also participate.

"Interact with the dog in a consistent way from the beginning. Be reasonable, be fair, and don't teach the dog rough games," advises Dr. Nicholas Dodman, director of the Behavior Clinic at Tufts University School of Veterinary Medicine.

A New Baby

What do you do when the new arrival is not a dog—it's a baby? Perhaps you, your spouse, and the family dog have lived together for several years. Your dog may be convinced that it's the center of your universe. You take it for long walks, brush it twice a week, and scratch its ears and rub its belly on demand. How will your dog behave when a new baby steals the limelight? You can avoid potential behavior problems by changing your dog's routine before the new baby's arrival so your dog does not think the baby is the cause of upheaval and change.

If you have been overly indulgent, now is the time to scale back. Train (or retrain) your dog in basic obedience. "Train your dog to 'say please' and to have good manners. Make it earn your attention," advises Dr. Dodman.

Will the new baby cause changes in your dog's walking schedule? Perhaps mom has always taken Rover for an early morning walk, but dad will soon be doing dawn patrol. Before the baby is due, allow your dog a few weeks to settle into this new walking routine.

You may also want to push an empty baby stroller as you walk the dog. Soon your dog will grow accustomed to the strange device with its clattering wheels.

Has your dog ever heard a baby's cry? If it hasn't, it may be afraid or overly curious when it suddenly hears strange noises coming from the baby's room. Ask a friend with an infant to make a recording of the baby's crying. Play the tape at home on an irregular schedule to accustom your dog to the new sound.

Set up the baby's room several weeks before the due date. If you plan to put up a gate in the doorway, put it up now, then deny the dog access to the room. Buy the baby powders and lotions you intend to use and sprinkle a bit on your wrist so your dog becomes familiar with the new smell.

When the baby is born, dad should bring home an article of the baby's clothing or a blanket with the baby's scent on it before mom and baby return from the hospital. Let your dog sniff the article to become familiar with the baby's scent.

Welcome Home

By the time the big day arrives, your dog should be well prepared to meet the new member of the family. Carefully orchestrate the first meeting. Not having seen mom for a few days, Rover will probably be waiting inside the door with an enthusiastic welcome; so dad should wait outside with the baby and let mom enter first.

After mom has calmed the dog, she should put it on a lead. Be sure the dog is sitting peacefully before dad enters with the baby. If the dog shows an interest in the baby, allow the dog to approach while one parent holds the baby and the other holds the dog's lead. In most instances, the dog will sniff a bit to satisfy its curiosity and then go about its business. But be prepared to halt the introduction if your dog shows signs of fear or aggression.

In the weeks that follow, include the dog in your activities while the baby is awake. Give the dog its familiar commands—"sit," "down," "stay"—and reward it with food treats or a pat on the head. When the baby is asleep, withdraw special attention from the dog. Rover will quickly learn that nice things happen when the baby is around.

Danger Signs

A frightened or aggressive dog displays warning signs that another dog would understand but that people often overlook or misinterpret. When introducing a new dog to children, closely watch the dog for signs of fear or aggression. And teach children to recognize the warning signs as soon as they are old enough to understand.

A fearful dog may flatten its ears against its head and put its tail between its legs. It may also lower the front half of its body and retreat. Tell your children never to touch or approach a fearful dog and not to chase the dog if it runs or hides. A fearful dog may bite if it thinks it is being pursued or cornered.

A dog may become aggressive for several reasons: out of fear, because it feels you are invading its territory, or because it is an unusually dominant dog. If a dog exposes its teeth or growls, it is telling you it is about to bite.

If your dog growls or bares its teeth at a child, keep the dog separated from children and seek professional help. Correcting an aggression problem is not a do-it-yourself job. Ask your veterinarian to recommend an animal behaviorist or experienced animal trainer who can work with your dog.

Domestic Harmony

The effort you invest in choosing a dog and carefully introducing it to your children will pay years of rewards. Dogs want to know their

place in our social hierarchy, and they want to please us. When your dog shows respect for all members of the family and your children have learned to treat the dog with gentleness, you have created the foundation for years of happiness together. ❧

5

Sleeping Dogs...

Sleep is vital to a dog's mental and physical well-being, maintaining their immune systems, aiding memory and recharging their batteries.

Have you ever noticed how much your dog sleeps? Counting "catnaps" and longer snoozes, dogs average about 14 hours of sleep each day. And how your pooch sleeps could affect how well you sleep—because 59 percent of dog owners share bedrooms with their sleep-happy canines, according to a recent survey by the American Animal Hospital Association.

Why Sleep?

Dogs have so much fun while they're awake, it's a wonder they care to sleep at all. "Sleep seems to be overwhelmingly important to an animal's physical and mental health, though," says Dr. Bruce Fogle, a London-based veterinarian and author of *The Dog's Mind.* Experts theorize that sleep recharges Bowser's batteries, and also helps his brain sort out memories of the day's events.

Sleep also appears to bolster dogs' immune systems. Animals can eventually die from lack of sleep, more specifically, from immune-system dysfunction caused by sleep deprivation.

Comfort Zones

Dogs are inveterate comfort seekers, and their quest for comfort influences where and when they plop down to catch 40 winks. Wild dogs sleep in dens, and their domestic counterparts also favor a sheltered sleeping spot that feels like a den—hence the under-the-bed or under-the-table sleeping habits of many domestic dogs. Before your dog lies down, it may circle around or paw at its sleeping spot—an innate behavior that simulates carving out a denlike depression in the ground.

How protective a dog is of its "nest" can reveal how dominant the dog is. In the wild, the "top dog" usually sleeps "wherever he wants," says Dr. Stanley Coren, professor of psychology at the University of British Columbia in Canada. So if your dog responds with a growl when you approach its sleeping area, you may need to modify your interactions with Rover (with veterinary guidance) to reestablish your leadership position.

WILD DOGS SLEEP IN DENS, AND THEIR DOMESTIC COUNTERPARTS ALSO FAVOR A SHELTERED SLEEPING SPOT THAT FEELS LIKE A DEN—HENCE THE UNDER-THE-BED OR UNDER-THE-TABLE SLEEPING HABITS OF MANY DOMESTIC DOGS.

Biological Clocks

The interplay between two hormones produced by your dog's nervous system affects sleepiness and wakefulness. One hormone, melatonin, secreted by the brain's pineal gland, surges to higher levels during nighttime hours, leading scientists to speculate that this hormone induces sleep. The second hormone, serotonin, helps your dog maintain alertness and muscle tone. While your dog is awake, certain nerve cells release serotonin by firing rapidly and consistently. But as these nerve cells fire less frequently, your dog gets drowsy; and when the nerve cells stop firing altogether, the dog sleeps deeply.

But hormones are not the exclusive mediators of slumber. Environmental conditions and instinctive behaviors also shape your dog's sleep-wake cycle. Your dog has a built-in circadian "clock" that seasonally adjusts the dog's sleep periods to changing patterns of daylight and darkness. And in spring and fall, unneutered domestic dogs typically sleep less because these are the seasons of peak reproductive activity. In addition, a dog's hunting instincts influence its sleep-wake patterns. Wild dogs and free-roaming domestic dogs are most active during hunting hours—dawn and dusk—and many family dogs are also "full of beans" at those times.

Dogs also coordinate nap times with their home life. Social animals that they are, they tend to be awake and alert when their people are up and about. But when left alone during the day, most well-adjusted dogs fall asleep because "nothing's doing."

Perchance to Dream...

Studies have shown that a dog's brain activity during rapid-eye-movement (REM) sleep is comparable to that of a human. In people, REM sleep is associated with dreaming. Although dogs can't tell us whether they dream, their physical behavior and brain patterns during REM sleep have led many people to surmise that dogs do dream.

A dog's muscles sometimes move during REM sleep—even though the muscles are in a state of relaxation. The dog's whiskers may twitch, its tail may thump, and its legs may paddle as if it's running. Barks and yips often accompany these movements. While Rover's vocalizations and body movements don't prove he's dreaming, we can easily imagine him hotly pursuing a fleeing squirrel in his sleep.

After 10 to 20 minutes of slow-wave sleep, the dog enters the REM phase. During the 5- to 7-minute REM stage, you may notice your dog's eyes moving rapidly under its closed lids. Vocalization and jerky muscle movements often accompany REM sleep Also during the REM stage, the dog's breathing becomes irregular and shallow; its brain activity simulates wakefulness; and its muscles become totally relaxed, mimicking paralysis.

Sleep Types and Cycles

As a dog becomes sleepy and relaxed, it often lies on its chest in a Sphinx-like position, with its legs tucked under its body and its head resting on its front paws. (Many dogs feel more secure with back support while they sleep, as owners who bunk with their dogs often find out.)

Dogs sleep more frequently during a 24-hour period than we do, but their sleep episodes are shorter. The average dog's sleep-wake cycle lasts about 20 to 30 minutes (compared to the average human cycle of 90 minutes). But the length of the cycle "varies according to the animal's size," notes Dr. Coren,. A large mastiff may clock a 40-minute cycle, while a diminutive Yorkie's sleep cycle may be just 15 minutes.

Cycle length notwithstanding, the same situations that make us drowsy make our dogs feel that way, too: a full stomach, a quiet house, the aftermath of vigorous exercise, or a warm patch of sunshine.

Moreover, the content of a dog's sleep is much the same as ours. There is a slow-wave or "quiet" phase and a rapid-eye-movement (REM) or "active" phase.

During slow-wave sleep, a dog lies still, oblivious to its surroundings. Its breathing slows and deepens, its blood pressure and body temperature drop, and its heart and metabolic rate slow down. Simultaneously, the dog's brainwaves (as measured by an electroencephalogram) settle into a pattern that is much more rhythmic than the fluctuating brainwave pattern of wakefulness.

During REM sleep, dogs usually curl into a furry ball or lie on their side. The occasional dog that sleeps on its back during REM sleep is extraordinarily self-confident and comfortable with its surroundings.

Once you determine your dog's favorite sleeping position, you'll be able to select the most suitable size and shape of dog bed for your chum.Left undisturbed, dogs typically emerge from REM sleep on their own, then fall back into slow-wave sleep. But a dog that's suddenly aroused from REM sleep may snap or snarl, which lends some credence to the maxim, "Let sleeping dogs lie."

Keep in mind that an adult dog's sleep patterns are not the same as a very young dog's. During the first few weeks of life, when a puppy's brain is developing rapidly, REM sleep dominates. By the time a pup reaches about 4 months of age, however, its sleep patterns practically match those of an adult—about one-quarter REM and the rest slow-wave sleep.

Sleep Disorders

Sleep disorders are uncommon in dogs, but they do occur. Narcolepsy—an inherited condition seen most often in Doberman pinschers, Labrador retrievers, beagles, and poodles—is characterized by sudden bouts of sleep at inappropriate times, such as during play or mealtimes. Cataplexy (sudden loss of muscle control and resulting collapse) often accompanies narcolepsy. Scientists don't know exactly what causes narcolepsy, but the condition can be managed (though not cured) with medication. If you suspect your dog has narcolepsy, videotape its behavior at home and show the video to your veterinarian. Although narcoleptics collapse frequently at home, they rarely exhibit this behavior at animal clinics.

Sleep apnea is a condition in which a dog intermittently stops breathing while sleeping because its soft palate blocks its airway. Dogs with the condition don't sleep soundly because their slumber is frequently interrupted as they gasp for air. Snoring is common with sleep apnea, but not all dogs that snore have this disorder. Obese dogs are predisposed to sleep apnea because their soft palate may enlarge with fat buildup. Sleep apnea is also fairly common in short-nosed (brachycephalic) dogs like bulldogs and pugs because their soft palates are often oversized.

Dr. Joan Hendricks, professor of medicine at the University of Pennsylvania School of Veterinary Medicine, has seen a sleeping bulldog stop breathing as many as 110 times in one hour! Although Dr. Hendricks is investigating medications to help relieve sleep apnea, the current treatment of choice is surgery to trim the soft palate.

In REM behavior disorder, a sleeping dog in the rapid-eye-movement (REM) phase of sleep does not experience the muscle relaxation typical of REM sleep. Instead, the dog thrashes about wildly even though he's fast asleep. Since dogs can injure themselves in this state, so scientists are exploring biochemical treatments for this disorder.

Thankfully, most dogs aren't insomniacs. But some dogs manage to train their owners to let them out for a wee-hour "tinkle." By giving in to these demands, owners of such dogs only reinforce such nocturnal behavior.

However, dogs do sometimes develop medical conditions (such as kidney disease or diabetes) that make it necessary for them to relieve themselves in the middle of the night. And the sleep patterns of even a healthy dog may change as it ages. In general, older dogs tend to sleep for shorter periods and may become restless between snoozes. (If your dog's sleep patterns change suddenly, though, play it safe and consult your veterinarian.)

Your dog's snoring can disrupt its sleep (not to mention yours if Rover is "sawing wood" in close proximity to you). Snoring often comes with aging. Older dogs lose elasticity in their soft palates (the fleshy partition at the back of their mouths), which can lead to a partial airway blockage that sets off snoring. But certain brachycephalic breeds like pugs and boxers often start snoring early in life due to their short noses and contorted airways. ❁

6

Dog Talk

Dogs bark in many different situations and to express many different emotional states, including fear, distress, desire, and joy.

Dogs have many ways of communicating with one another and with us. Among their oft-used communication tools is vocalization. Growls, whines, and howls convey a range of meanings from one dog to another. But the bark—the most common canine utterance—seems to be directed mainly to humans. Most experts suspect canines do not communicate with each other by barking because wolves and coyotes, the dog's "next of kin," rarely bark. (When they do, it's only in stressful situations.)

Nevertheless, most dogs have a "hard wired" barking instinct. And they do use it. Some surmise that early breeders selected specifically for "alarm barking." Others believe ancient people bred dogs for tameness—and barking came along with the genetic package. Regardless of how it evolved, barking is often tricky for humans to interpret because dogs bark in many situations and emotional states, including fear, distress, desire, and joy.

Different Kinds of Barking

■ Spontaneous Barking

Many dogs bark spontaneously when stressed or stimulated. Some, for example, emit a low-pitched warning or a higher-pitched welcome when "aliens" tread on their turf. Then, of course, there's the invitational "let's play!" bark and the call-and-response "barkathon," where one barker sets off a chain of barking.

■ Learned Barking

Whether they intend to or not, owners often encourage barking. If you reward your dog's vocal response to a "speak" command with treats, for example, your pooch will soon associate barking with tasty tidbits and will bark repetitively to get them. (Who's training whom?)

Similarly, if your dog's insistent "let me in" bark prompts you to open the door, the dog will learn that barking loudly and long enough will get results. Surprisingly, yelling "be quiet" at a barking dog may actually reinforce its barking behavior. "For many dogs, any kind of attention is rewarding—even reprimands," says Dr. Nicholas Dodman. Just as one barking dog incites others to chime in, one "barking" human can also encourage dogs to vocalize too much.

Sometimes, "innocent bystanders" reinforce barking. If your dog barks at the letter carrier who then leaves after dropping off the mail, the dog probably figures it has done a good job of scaring off an intruder.

If you've inadvertently taught your dog to bark too much, you'll have to modify your behavior to prevent excessive barking from continuing. Don't do anything Fifi or Fido could perceive as encouragement for barking. In fact, make sure you reward your dog for not barking or for stopping on command.

■ Home-Alone Barking

Alas, some dogs bark simply because there's nothing else to do. "Repetitive, monotonous barking is often a response to isolation," notes Dr. Dodman.

Separation anxiety can also trigger excessive barking. Some dogs are so overcome with anxiety when their owners leave that barking helps relieve the stress. There are a few things you can do to help a dog with separation anxiety. "Cool" your relationship with the dog, train it to keep quiet as you gradually lengthen periods of separation, and vigorously exercise it before you leave for any extended period

■ Bothersome Barkers

While dog owners usually don't mind some barking, excessive barking is a nuisance. Owner definitions of "acceptable" barking vary according to their living situation and their neighbors' noise tolerance. In general, though, "if a dog won't stop barking when you tell it to, you have a problem," says Dennis Fetko, Ph.D., a California-based animal behaviorist.

Because barking is innately programmed behavior and excessive barking can become so entrenched, "treatment" for barking requires patience and persistence. The first step is to identify what incites your dog's vocalization. You can then usually silence the dog by eliminating or modifying the stimulus. Remember, though, if you want your dog to bark in certain situations, you should aim to control barking, not eliminate it. (Reward your dog when it vocalizes appropriately so it learns when it's OK to bark.)

If your canine is a chronic barker out of doors, try bringing it inside. Most healthy adult dogs can stay indoors for about 8 hours with no problem. But if your dog has been banished outdoors because of indoor indiscretions such as housesoiling, you'll have to address the original behavior problem before you bring your dog inside.

■ Bred to Bark

Beagles and several terrier breeds top the "Barker List." Fox hunters selectively bred beagles to bark as they led the way to the fox. And the bygone "profession" of terriers was to alert hunters to the location of rodent burrows, which carries over today in the insistent barking of many terriers.

Nip Barking in the Bud

You can forestall excessive barking in several ways. First, when selecting a breed, consider the typically nonreactive, "low volume" breeds such as bulldogs or Old English sheepdogs. Second, never reward your dog for any unwanted vocalization. Finally, be sure to meet your dog's needs for exercise and mental stimulation. Dogs that are physically and mentally tired are less likely to bark.

■ Unearth the Cause

If you try to solve problem barking but overlook what sets it off, your dog may become silent but still show its stress through other vexing "coping mechanisms" like destructive chewing or digging.

■ Sitting Silently

Treating chronic barking can be easier if you and your dog have a handle on basic obedience. If you're present when Fifi is barking inappropriately, try to hush her up by commanding a sit-stay. (Enforced mental concentration often distracts dogs from barking.) Once she is sitting, give a quiet but firm "cease" or "enough" command. After several seconds of silence, praise her calmly—not effusively.

You'll need to retrain your dog if it erupts into incessant barking at the mere sound of a knock or doorbell. Start by having an accomplice ring the doorbell or knock. Let your dog bark twice or thrice as a reward for alerting you. Then give it a "quiet" or "cease" command and praise it for quieting down before you open the door and greet your visitor. If your dog stays silent, let your friend reward the dog with a food treat.

Problems with Punishment

Punishment is an unpleasant but not harsh consequence of undesirable behavior that is meant to decrease the behavior's frequency. Properly selected and applied, punishment can help temporarily curb barking. It does, however, have drawbacks.

Punishment rarely addresses the underlying cause of the barking, and it needs to be applied consistently to work well. If a dog does not receive a correction for each and every barking episode, these "unpunished" barking incidents will reinforce barking in general.

When you witness the barking "crime," you can toss a clattering shake can (an empty soda can containing a dozen coins) near your dog. But don't let your dog see you toss it because punishment is more effective if a dog can't tell where it's coming from. Bark-activated collars that deliver an unpleasant (but harmless) shock or a whiff of citronella have pluses and minuses. When the dog is wearing the collar, the collar usually administers consistent corrections, but when it is removed, the dog sometimes starts barking again. Another drawback: when the dog is wearing the collar, the animal may not bark at all. And some alarm barking may be a good thing.

In the final analysis, most animal behaviorists recommend punishment for excessive barking only as an adjunct to other techniques. And for certain behavior problems such as fears and phobias, punishment is definitely counterproductive. ❧

Section II

Social Hierarchy

7

The Family Pack

Your dog perceives your family as a "pack"
so it accords you and other family members
the social status of colleagues.

Veteran dog watchers know that dogs like to be where their people are and do what their people do. Their natural sociability makes dogs peerless companions and beloved family members. Your dog, however, perceives the family as a "pack," so it accords you and other family members the social status of colleagues.

Wolf Packs

Most animal behaviorists believe that the wolf (Canis lupus) is the modern domesticated dog's direct ancestor, so understanding wolf behavior may help us figure out what makes our dogs tick. For wolves, communal living is a matter of survival. Wolf packs typically consist of a half-dozen, often blood-related individuals. To feed themselves efficiently, members of wolf packs hunt cooperatively. Packs also work together to establish and protect hunting territory and dens through urine marking, howling, and aggression toward intruders. To help maintain social harmony, the pack organizes itself into a dominance hierarchy—a pyramid of submissive "underdogs," "middle rankers" (a mix of up-and-coming juveniles and mature wolves), and one top dog—the "alpha wolf."

A "law of the pack" limits breeding to two wolves—often the most dominant male and female. When breeding season approaches, dominant wolves increasingly exhibit rank-clarifying behavior such as posturing, snapping, and snarling. Such demonstrations reinforce dominance relationships and send a clear message to lower-ranking wolves not to mate. But subordinate nonbreeding pack members don't seem to hold any grudges; on the contrary, they often babysit pups while mom rests or hunts.

The dominance hierarchy helps promote the greatest good for the greatest number, but it is not inflexible. According to Dr. Nicholas Dodman, director of the Behavior Clinic at Tufts University School of Veterinary Medicine, "Relationships may change depending on the situation and individual motivation." The leaders of the hunt, for example, may not be the same wolves that mate. And possession is sometimes "nine-tenths of lupine law." For example, a hungry subordinate wolf gnawing on a bone may growl at a more dominant wolf hovering nearby. If the higher-ranking wolf has already eaten (dominant wolves usually get first dibs on food), it may back off and allow the underling to keep its prize.

Aside from the occasional dominance tussle, wolves are, by and large, amiable. Even the most dominant pack members communicate primarily with nonviolent body signals and vocalizations. "Hurting one another doesn't make biological sense, because injured animals can't breed or hunt," explains Dr. Petra A. Mertens, a veterinary resident at the Behavior Clinic of Tufts University School of Veterinary Medicine. Friendliness and affection is certainly evident in the typical wolf-pack greeting ceremony—a muzzle-licking, tail-wagging expression of canine joy that reaffirms pack solidarity.

Dogs, Not Wolves

Despite many behavioral similarities between wolves and dogs (for example, your dog's gleeful dance when you return home is the dog version of the wolf greeting ceremony), experts warn against extending comparisons too far. "Dog social behavior is much less well-defined and less stereotyped than that of wolves," says Dr. Benson Ginsburg, head of the Behavior Genetics Laboratory at the University of Connecticut. "Today's dog recombines bits and pieces of wolf behavior but does not display the whole working pattern." ˎ

The dog's more fragmented social behavior evolved as humankind selectively bred dogs for certain physical and temperamental characteristics. Most experts equate the typical adult dog's social and intellectual maturity with that of an immature wolf. While this "arrested development" facilitates bonding between people and dogs, it can make dog behavior more difficult to interpret than wolf behavior. "Wolves communicate clearly what their intentions are," says Dr. Ginsburg. "That's not necessarily true of domesticated dogs.

"What's more, a dog's social behavior is affected by the changeable human environment it lives in. Wolves have an easier time establishing behavioral standards because their society is more homogeneous. "When a social organization is as dynamic as the average family today, the 'rules' are constantly changing," observes Dr. Dodman. For example, dogs sometimes get confused about where they fit in when a new baby arrives. To prevent this sort of role confusion, behaviorists emphasize that family members need to be as consistent as possible with their dogs.

"...A DOG'S SOCIAL BEHAVIOR IS
AFFECTED BY THE CHANGEABLE HUMAN
ENVIRONMENT IT LIVES IN."
DR. BENSON GINSBURG

Nature and Nurture

Your dog certainly has the genetic potential for social behavior (inherited from its wolf ancestors), but a dog needs certain experiences to nurture this potential. A puppy's earliest interactions with its mother and littermates help it learn the basic rules of "canine etiquette." When a rambunctious pup gets on mom's nerves, it often sees a lifted maternal lip, hears a throaty growl, and sometimes may find itself airborne—lifted by the scruff of its neck. Also, playing with littermates gives puppies practice in social behaviors that come in handy later on. Puppies learn, for example, to distinguish head-down/fanny-up play bows from more threatening postures

Because so much important "body language" learning and practice takes place during this time, pups should stay with one another and with their mother for at least 7 or 8 weeks. The social and communication skills dogs derive from this period of close contact may prevent later behavior problems between dogs.

IF YOU ALLOW YOUR DOG TO SLEEP ON
YOUR BED—OR ASSUME ANY POSITION
THAT NEGATES YOUR HEIGHT ADVANTAGE—
YOUR DOG MAY FEEL MORE DOMINANT.

Understanding Dominance

Dominance behavior among wolves is a survival mechanism that provides social cement for the pack. But dominant behavior in domesticated dogs can sometimes cause problems within the family. Understanding how dogs exhibit and perceive dominance can help owners cope with inappropriate displays of dominance—the most serious of which is aggression (growling, snarling, and biting).

Dominant dogs insist on initiating most of the activities they engage in. A dog's reluctance to move from the chair you want to sit in also betrays a dominant attitude. And dominant dogs can get very possessive about food—or anything else they have in or near their mouths. Moreover, people sometimes unknowingly reinforce their dog's dominant status. For example, if you allow your dog to sleep on your bed—or assume any position that negates your height advantage—your dog may feel more dominant.

If your dog growls or attempts to bite you when you groom it, pat it, reclaim its food dish, or give it a "sit" or "down" command, consider seeking advice from your veterinarian or get a referral to an animal behaviorist. Most professionals coach owners of dominant-aggressive dogs to reward the dog's submissive behavior and ignore—not confront— its bossiness.

One way owners exert "natural" dominance over their dogs is by controlling access to the food supply. (Some owners reinforce this by commanding their dog to "sit and stay" before putting the food bowl down.) Whenever your dog promptly obeys your command, it is recognizing your position as "top dog"—at least for the moment.

Your dog, like you, is an individual not a robot; and its social behavior may fluctuate as situations change. So, make every effort to interact with your dog in ways that maintain your leadership; at the same time, foster good will among all members of the family pack.

Body Language

"If only my dog could talk," most dog owners have fantasized. Actually, your dog can "talk"—but to understand, you need to know how to "listen" to its body language.

Dogs use their bodies to convey their state of mind and their rank in group situations. Dominant dogs carry their ears, hackles, and tails up; stand stiffly; and stare self-confidently. If challenged, they may show their teeth or growl. A dominant dog usually approaches its submissive counterpart at a right angle and may attempt to place its muzzle or paw over the underdog's shoulder.

Conversely, submissive dogs keep their ears down and back, avert their eyes, and crouch with their tails low or between their legs. Active submission occurs when a dog rolls over on its back, exposing its belly. (But beware: a dog that assumes this posture just so you'll scratch its belly may not be a submissive dog.)

Because the behavior of most dogs lies somewhere between these body-language extremes, it's important to look at the whole picture when "reading" your dog. "You can't rely on the eyes or ears or tail alone," says Dr. Petra A. Mertens, a veterinary resident at the Behavior Clinic of Tufts University School of Veterinary Medicine. For example, a dog in a play bow may bark loudly, but the posture tells you that the vocalization is nonthreatening. (Dogs, like their wolf cousins, are never too old to play.) And a fearful dog may show signs of both submission (tail tucked or wagging, ears back) and aggression (hackles up, teeth bared). Whenever the front and rear ends of a dog convey different messages, pay attention to the end that's most potentially harmful.

Selective breeding for features such as floppy ears and short snouts (not to mention "cosmetic" surgical alterations) makes it harder for some dogs to communicate using stereotyped canine body postures. In a recent study of Cavalier King Charles spaniels, researchers observed that the dogs exhibited no visual signaling with eyes, ears, hackles, or tails. Instead, they used movement to maintain their hierarchical relationships; the more dominant members of the group pushed their way past the more submissive dogs.

Don't forget that dogs are also constantly reading our body language. And—as with our reading of dogs—there is sometimes misunderstanding. For instance, if you stare at a particularly beautiful dog, it might perceive your rapture as a challenge to its dominance and react aggressively. And some dogs interpret any human position over or above them as dominance. While many dogs love a good cuddle, a few perceive even innocuous gestures—such as hugs, grooming, or a pat on the head—as challenges to their rank—and these dogs may respond aggressively. ❧

8

Your Pooch's Place

The pack mentality imbues dogs with a sense of responsibility toward those with whom they live —including humans.

It's a well-known fact that dogs like to know where they stand in the social order. Wild dogs arrange themselves in social hierarchies known as packs—with dominant top dogs, middle rankers, and submissive underdogs. This social structure helps them hunt efficiently, protect their young and their territory, and settle internal disputes with minimal fighting.

The canine "pack mentality" also affects how family dogs relate to their people. "Dogs don't see us as two-legged dogs, but they do enter into pack-like relationships with us," says Dr. Gerry Flannigan, a resident at Tufts University School of Veterinary Medicine's Behavior Clinic. This canine concept of social order makes dogs great family companions. It also makes dogs amenable to working cooperatively with people—be it herding sheep, protecting our homes, or assisting those afflicted with disabilities.

In any social group, communication among individuals is key. Sending clear social messages to your dog and accurately interpreting its responses help create an orderly bispecies family "pack." Along with easy-to-read body-language messages, dogs give more subtle cues that owners often misread. For example, if your dog insists on putting its paws or head on your shoulders, it may be asserting dominance rather than showering you with affection. And while many people interpret canine smooches as expressions of love, in "dogspeak," face licking is how puppies request regurgitated food from mature dogs. Face licking is also a sign of submission to more dominant dogs and people.

TRULY DOMINANT DOGS RARELY FIGHT
BECAUSE THEY HAVE NOTHING TO PROVE.

Who's Leading Whom?

Most dogs are quite content to let the owner be the pack leader. But, a dog with dominant tendencies might attempt a "coup" if it perceives a lack of human leadership—for example, if the owner lets it get away with not obeying commands. "The dog might then think, 'This group needs a leader, so I'll be it,'" explains Dr. Flannigan.

Dogs use body language to communicate their position within the pack. A dominant dog makes direct eye contact and holds its ears and tail erect. If challenged, it raises its hackles, growls, and bares its teeth. A submissive dog avoids eye contact, lowers its head, flattens its ears, and tucks its tail.

Tough Love

If your dog refuses to obey commands, behaves protectively toward food or resting places, or—more seriously—growls at or nips family members, you may have a dominance problem on your hands. Consider implementing a "no free lunch" policy where your dog must work for everything it wants—food, toys, even attention. For example, before permitting the dog to eat, command it to sit or lie down. If your dog does not comply, don't feed it and walk away.

Physically or verbally punishing a dominant dog is unwise because it will view such behavior as a di-

rect challenge and may react aggressively. Instead, take a less confrontational approach. For starters, keep your dog off your bed. Dogs allowed to sleep on their owner's bed sometimes view the privilege as proof of exalted status and try to take further advantage. "Demote" your pooch to its own, comfortable bed—on the floor.

To reassert your leadership with an overly dominant dog, give the dog food, access to the outdoors, and attention only after it obeys a command. Be patient: relegating a dominant dog to middle-rank status relative to you can take about 2 months. And be careful: some dominant dogs are very aggressive, so you may need help from an animal behaviorist.

Sidestepping Obstacles

To avoid or minimize behavioral problems related to social status, you should consider gender and breed when choosing a dog. Males, generally larger and stronger than females of the same breed, are more likely to be dominant. However, large size alone does not always translate into dominance; many dachshunds and Chihuahuas, for example, try to lord it over a dog—or an owner—several times their size. And while some breeds—such as huskies, schnauzers, and boxers—are predisposed toward dominance, Dr. Flannigan notes that "dogs are individuals, and there are dominant individuals in every breed." You can also reduce the likelihood of dominance-related problems by not engaging your dog in rough-and-tumble games like wrestling and tug-of-war.

■ Pack Destabilizers
Changing social circumstances can disrupt an otherwise stable family "pack." A newly arrived puppy might usurp the top-dog status of an elderly incumbent. Or the death of an older dog might embolden a once-submissive canine survivor to become more assertive. The birth of a baby and the arrival or departure of other human family members can also alter pack dynamics.

Puppyhood is the ideal time to introduce a dog into your family. Before selecting a pup, watch littermate interactions. But be aware that although pups develop their rank in the litter hierarchy between the ages of 4 and 6 weeks, their social status is not etched in stone at this young age. Depending on their subsequent experiences with other dogs and people, some puppies that exhibit submissive behavior early on develop dominant tendencies later in life—and vice versa.

■ Status Changes

Dr. Flannigan notes that a dog's social system is more fluid than animal behaviorists once thought. So it's important to monitor your dog's place in the family hierarchy—especially when life-changing events occur—and reassert your leadership if necessary. Happily, most dog-dog or dog-human pack disputes can be settled with gentle but unwavering guidance from you—the leader of the pack.

Is More Merrier?

Social dynamics become a bit more complex in families with more than one dog. If your multiple-dog household consists of dogs raised together from puppyhood, your pets probably adhere to pack positions established during littermate or parent-pup interactions. But when two or more unrelated dogs come together to live in the same family, the hierarchy might take time to sort itself out. In the process, canine power struggles sometimes ensue. Says Dr. Flannigan, "Dog fights usually occur when two dogs are at similar levels in the social hierarchy. Truly dominant dogs rarely fight because they have nothing to prove." Gender plays a role here also. Males and females are less likely to grapple with one another than are females with other females or males with other males.

If your dogs become embroiled in a pack spat (termed sibling rivalry—even if the dogs are not related by blood), determine which dog initiates the dog-dog interactions, because that dog is naturally "in charge." Support that dog. That means greeting the top dog first, feeding it first, and reprimanding the underdog if it tries to usurp the top spot.

Thankfully, most canine "disagreements" over rank don't result in bloodshed. Therefore, it's often best to let two dogs settle things by themselves—as long as "negotiations" are limited to nonharming body language and vocalizations. Occasionally, however, sibling rivalry escalates into violence that calls for definitive human intervention. If the natural but belligerent underdog is an intact male, neutering may help reinforce the social distinction. "And if two dogs can't work out their places in the hierarchy without endangering each other, they should be separated," says Dr. Flannigan.

The pack mentality imbues dogs with a sense of responsibility toward those with whom they live—including humans. This canine cooperativeness helps people train dogs to perform a wide array of human-helpful tasks.

For example, a dog trained to assist deaf people will alert its owner if it hears the phone ring, a baby crying, a knock at the door, or a smoke alarm. "We train hearing dogs to assume a certain amount of authority," explains Dr. Bruce Fogle, a London-based veterinarian, author, and cofounder of Hearing Dogs for Deaf People in the U.K. But unchecked assertiveness can result in uncooperative, pushy canine behavior.

To help deaf owners maintain canine control, "we teach dogs to distinguish between circumstances in which they are leaders and others in which they must be followers," says Dr. Fogle. Prior to final placement in homes, dogs spend a week working with their prospective owners at a training center. There, hearing-dog owners learn to assert their leadership, applying straightforward obedience-training techniques. ❖

9

Dominant Dog:
Controlling Sibling Rivalry

It's a form of power struggle among dogs.
But determining which one is dominant is key
to keeping peace in the home.

"Oh no, the dogs are at it again!" Sound—and look—familiar? You've just come home after a hard day's work and instead of greeting you happily, your two dogs begin attacking each other. You rescue the puppy and hold it in your lap, checking for bite marks while driving off the larger, older pet, "Bad dog!"

When it's dinner time, the impatient puppy's whining prompts you to feed him first; once he's occupied, you feed the older dog, who's barking furiously at the puppy.

At bedtime, the puppy hops up onto the pillow next to you—isn't he cute—but when the older dog jumps onto to the bed, you direct him to the floor, and he growls unhappily. When the pup returns to the floor, jawing and scuffling break out.

What you've got is a classic case of sibling rivalry on your hands. Sibling rivalry in dogs does not necessarily refer to fighting between actual littermates, but is commonly defined as fighting between two or more dogs that reside in the same household resulting in injuries. Not surprisingly, it is one of the most common problems dog behaviorists are asked to treat and one of the trickier to resolve. All too frequently, owners are not aware that how they interact with their dogs can trigger the fighting.

"Sibling rivalry is a form of power struggle between dogs," says Dr. Nicholas Dodman author of *The Dog Who Loved Too Much: Tales, Treatments, and the Psychology of Dogs.* "Fighting is usually triggered by competition for something the dominant dog takes as his right, but which the other dog refuses to give up. Interference by the owner," he warns, "only insures that the fighting will continue." So, when you pull a puppy away from a more mature and larger dog because you feel sorry for the smaller dog, you're fueling rather than cooling their rivalry.

Pack Behavior

Introducing a new dog to the household can be a delicate matter. By treating a new dog in the household or a puppy as equal to—or even superior to—an older dog, you sow the seeds for sibling rivalry. Humans often attempt to equalize things between two or more dogs in the household, which goes against the dogs' natural instincts. As descendants of wolves, dogs follow a hierarchy: there is always a dominant dog in the pack, and the subordinate dogs naturally defer to it.

Dominance is not a bad thing—it's a natural behavior and it needs to be understood by dogs and people. Dominance is a way of insuring survival for the individual. It tends to be expressed by competition over resources and self-protection. Competition over resources, which can also be described as possessiveness, is seen frequently over food, but also toys, favored resting spots, and sometimes even for people and their attention. Even a pat on the head can result in self-protective responses such as growling and snapping. If you want a dominant dog to do something it doesn't want to, it may respond with a growl or even a bite. Such dogs need their space and you should respect that, even as you try to negotiate their pack rivalries.

Within any wolf pack, there are well-negotiated and respected hierarchies. When the hierarchy is stable, fighting is relatively uncommon. Then you throw humans, with their far more complex outlook on dominance and aggression, into the mix. Working out hierarchies for domestic dogs can become much more complicated than working them out in wolf packs. Breed, age and personality differences come into play and, most importantly, how you interact with your dogs.

Even before you select another dog for your home, you need to consider how your present dog will get along. According to Dr. Alice Moon, an assistant professor of animal behavior genetics at Tufts who has spent more than 20 years studying wolf pack behavior, "You bring home another dog who's a different breed; the two dogs might not get along. Given a choice, they might not want to live together. For example, say you have a nice, mellow shepherd cross and you bring home an aggressive terrier. All hell may break loose."

Some breeds, including certain types of spaniels and terriers, have a tendency to be aggressive and easily excitable. "They're the dominant wannabees," says Dr. Dodman. And they can cause all sorts of trouble when other, less dominant dogs are in the household. Two potentially aggressive dogs will need to establish an internal pecking order and that may take some tusseling, but after that there should be no ongoing problem. Dogs with less compatible temperaments, however, may face ongoing sibling rivalry.

ALL TOO FREQUENTLY, OWNERS ARE NOT AWARE THAT HOW THEY INTERACT WITH THEIR DOGS CAN TRIGGER THE FIGHTING.

Human Interference

In the wild, communication among members of a wolf pack is pretty straightforward. They have very clear survival needs, and the rules of relationships are established very early in life to those ends. Humans get in the way in dogs' lives. Dr. Moon says, "Wolves speak the same language, have the same goals. They settle things on their own, but in a household, owners are always intervening."

Sometimes, though, your quick intervention is important. You should try to defuse a serious fight. Dogs with dangerously strained relationships need to be watched and separated before they begin to fight. Scuffling or boxing—when the dogs are up on their hind legs like kangaroos—often precedes actual fighting. "You can see and hear it coming," Diane Arrington, trainer and owner of Pet Perfect Academy of Behavioral Science in Dallas, Texas, says. "It's different from normal scuffling. I call it toxic scuffling. It sounds edgy; it makes you feel uncomfortable."

Always interrupt this kind of behavior. Distract the dogs rather than yell at them. A nonviolent approach works best. "If you are violent towards the dogs," Arrington says, "you can trigger a fight or make a fight worse." Instead, she urges owners to whistle, open a door, pick up a toy or the leash. Dogs are more prone to joy than anger and, just as with young children, positive sorts of distractions and reinforcement is generally much more effective in the long run than punishment. "Introduce something to make them wag their tails."

When dogs are fighting over who's dominant, the feud will continue until one dog is clearly established as the victor and the other as the vanquished. Constant interference from dog owners—their misguided efforts at equal treatment or even favoring the underdog—confuses the issue and prolongs the problem.

Instead, you need to determine which is the dominant dog, and support it. But just figuring out which dog is dominant is not as simple as it seems.

Don't assume that the dog initiating the attack is the dominant dog in the household. Attacks may actually be the product of a more fearful outlook. Watch for behaviors such as how resistant or compliant each dog is at obeying commands, where the dogs sleep, which dog leads when running and which dog begins barking at intruder noises.

Favor the Dominant Dog

The way to quell sibling unrest may be counterintuitive. Once the issue of which is the dominant dog has been settled, that "alpha" dog must be given favored treatment. The dominant dog gets greeted first, fed first, petted first and goes out the door first. "Basically," says Dr. Dodman, "the dominant dog should be treated with priority in all matters.

There are other important steps: Obedience training, lots of exercise, an evaluation by a behaviorist, and, in some cases, changing the dogs' diets to a low protein food with no artificial preservatives can all prove beneficial. Food allergies or too high a protein intake can provoke aggressiveness. Arrington says, "A woman whose bulldog would attack her every time she got into the car with it was amazed at the change in her dog's behavior after she switched its food. Within two days, she said, it was like a different dog."

Working on sibling rivalry along with leadership training can take from 8 to 12 weeks. You'll have to separate the dogs when you're not at home. The low ranking dog may have to stay in while the high ranker goes outside, for example. The high ranker should always precede the low ranker both out of and into the house.

Counterconditioning—re-creating a positive association between the dogs—is another useful strategy. "If you were walking down the street and every person with red hair slapped you and every blonde gave you an M & M, you'd quickly develop a very positive association with blondes," Arrington says. "We try to do the same thing with positively reinforcing the feuding dogs' association with each other." If they can be together, even for very short periods of time without growling or fighting, the dogs should be praised, petted, and given treats.

You may have to work on re-introducing the two feuding dogs. Sometimes they may have to be restrained in each other's presence. It may take a harness with trailer ropes in order for the two dogs to be in the same room together, but this gives you a way to keep the dog of low rank away from the higher ranking dog.

Meanwhile you should be reassuring the high ranker in a calm, conversational manner. When the high ranker sees and hears this, it will boost its confidence. You may have to enlist the assistance of a friend to bring in the low ranking dog for increasing periods of time to get them used to being together without fighting. When you've got it right, you'll often find that the situation calms down quickly.

Sometimes medication are a necessary adjunct to behavior mod-

When dogs are fighting over who's dominant, the feud will continue until one dog is clearly established as the victor and the other as the vanquished.

ification. Drugs that may be appropriate could include propanolol, buspirone, or Prozac-like medications that increase levels of serotonin. Dominance-related aggression is thought to be associated with fluctuating levels of serotonin. Serotonin-enhancing drugs have a profound anti-aggressive effect, enabling owners to quickly gain the upper hand.

Hidden Causes

There are many causes for sibling rivalry, some of which may not be apparent. These include accidental trauma—two dogs are running across the street, one gets hit by a car and when the first comes back to sniff the injured dog, it causes lasting associations with pain and fear. Or, two dogs are playing in the yard when the collar of one gets caught against the fence or a bush causing pain, fear, and bad associations with the other dog.

Displaced aggression—a dog attacks his house mate because he can't get at the mailman who he really wants to bite—is another cause of sibling rivalry.

Finding the source of the sibling rivalry will help you solve the problem. If the fighting starts as soon as you walk through the door, you're going to have to assert yourself as the leader of the pack. It can be hard to persuade dominant dogs that you are in charge, but that's the only solution to the problem.

You're not doing the dogs any favors by allowing them to view you as their chew toy. It's always healthy to remind them that you're the boss. Even very aggressive dogs will benefit. Wresting control back from a dominant dog is viewed with relief by the dog. "It's almost," says Dr. Dodman, "as if the dog is saying, 'Thank heavens! For a moment there, I thought I was the one who was in charge here.'"

Unless the dogs understand that you are the leader of the pack, they'll have no interest in trying to gain your approval. Start by getting the dogs off the furniture. Also control the food and make it clear that you do. Don't simply leave food in the dogs' bowls throughout the day. That shows them that you are in control of the assets. Owners who have difficulty asserting themselves over their dominant dogs should get assistance and training.

Recounting his work with the owners of an aggressive rottweiler named Rocky, Dr. Dodman urged them to order Rocky off the furniture with a firm command such as "off," and reward him with praise or petting. Petting, he notes, is an extremely potent reward, and can be rationed and provided only when a reward is due.

"Owners who pet dominant dogs indiscriminately are, unbeknownst to themselves, rewarding their dog for nothing," Dr. Dodman says. "These dogs have much less incentive to work for a reward." Adds Arrington: "Make the dogs earn any treat or praise. Humans have to earn their pay; for a dog, a biscuit is his paycheck."

Basic to the resolution of sibling rivalry is putting an end to all violence in the household. "Dogs mimic the behavior of humans," says Arrington. "The number one mistake dog owners make is thinking they can discipline fights away. It's useless to be violent towards your dogs."

Dr. Dodman agrees: "The best approach is to regard the dog as a child. Provide positive reinforcement of desired behaviors. Yelling 'No!' is usually ineffective, and physical punishment should never be necessary.

UNLESS THE DOGS UNDERSTAND THAT
YOU ARE THE LEADER OF THE PACK,
THEY'LL HAVE NO INTEREST IN TRYING TO
GAIN YOUR APPROVAL.

When Medication Is Warranted

Medication is a tool that may help to quell sibling rivalry. The new, psychoactive drugs can help calm aggressive behavior. In most cases they allow the problem dog to respond to behavior modification; in those cases when the behavior problem is serious enough that an owner is considering euthanasia, medication can be a life saver for a dog.

A useful class of medications for controlling aggressive behavior are the selective serotonin reuptake inhibitors (SSRIs) like Prozac, Zoloft, Paxil, and Luvox—in dog-size doses, of course. (If you're taking one of these prescription medications, don't even think about giving it to your dog! You need to check with a vet who can prescribe the correct dosage based on your dog's size, weight, and behavior problem.)

Medication, however, won't do the job alone. It is a tool to be used along with other tactics as part of an overall strategy of behavior modification: plenty of exercise, a sensible diet, maybe with some amino acid supplements, and behavior and environmental modification or enhancement. Give the dog something to do during the day.

Drugs can be used for as little as a month, or for a prolonged amount of time—four to six months in cases of severe sibling rivalry or dominance aggression. In some situations where the dog regresses if taken off the medication, you may be looking at dosing it for the rest of its life.

Cost depends on the drug, the size of the dog and the severity of the problem. Inderal, for example, can cost as little as a few cents per tablet, while Prozac starts at a couple of dollars per day for a medium size dog. While a very small dog's medication could cost less than a quarter per day, the cost of a Great Dane's daily medication could be as much as $10 per day.

Preventing Rivalries: Case Study

Thomas and Abby could have been a case study in sibling rivalry, but their owners' careful planning prevented confrontations when Thomas joined the household. Ten-year-old Abby, a golden retriever crossed with a red setter, was getting used to being an only dog after the death of her companion, 12-year-old Ben, a black Labrador, when her owners, Susan and Graeme Keir, acquired Thomas.

Thomas, a high-energy six-month-old male mixed breed was lucky to join a household where the owners had lots of experience with dogs. Susan was a humane educator with the Massachusetts Society for the Prevention of Cruelty to Animals, and a volunteer at Angel Memorial Hospital for dogs and cats in Boston. "Thomas is a high-maintenance dog," says Graeme, "He wouldn't do well with an inexperienced owner."

Before bringing him home, Graeme and Susan visited with Thomas at the animal shelter in Hopkinton, MA. They spent time with him there, observing how the young dog interacted with the other dogs. Next, they brought Abby to the shelter for a visit. "We wanted them to meet on neutral ground," Susan explains. "Abby can be aggressive."

The Keirs' worries were allayed when Thomas immediately deferred to Abby. Once home, they took the dogs into the yard first before letting them inside the house. "Abby occasionally gave a quick, sharp bark, her reprimand bark," says Susan, "but that's as far as she went."

At first the Keirs kept Thomas in his crate during the day. He's a high-strung dog who'd been adopted and returned to the shelter three times before they acquired him. During the first few weeks, the Keirs would bring Thomas' crate into the living room with them and Abby.

"At first he couldn't sit with us—he was too excited— so we'd put him into the crate to calm him down." says Graeme. He and Susan took the dogs on long walks every day to help settle the young dog down.

After almost two years, Thomas and Abby are still getting along. Even when a guest visits, the two are more interested in their toys.

Once in a while Abby shows Thomas who's the boss, though. She takes his red, rubber ball, and though he looks longingly at it, he waits until she's finished before snatching it away. ❧

10

Dogs and Other Critters

*A responsible dog owner needs to understand the
dynamics of interspecies relationships,
both under the same roof and in the outside world.*

Surveys reveal that a large number of dog owners keep house
not only for canines but for other pets as well. Dogs in these
multispecies households find themselves in close proximity to everything from cats and guinea pigs to iguanas and
parrots. (Bowser is much less likely, however, to have close encounters with pets that live in dog-proof quarters, like cages.) In the
great outdoors, your dog may also come in contact with animals
owned by others.

A responsible dog owner therefore needs to understand the dynamics of interspecies relationships—both within the house and
outside among the neighborhood cats or Farmer Brown's cattle. Remember, you can be held liable for injuries your dog inflicts on other
people's pets. And, in several states, it's legal to kill a dog that attacks or "worries" livestock.

Despite the popular expression "fighting like cats and dogs," the
vast majority of animals living under the same roof have peaceful
relationships. Notes Dr. Nicholas Dodman, "For the most part, dogs
and other animals cohabit happily. Problems are more the excep-
tion than the rule." Most young animals—especially pups and kit-
tens—quickly develop congenial relationships with each other, often
becoming best buddies. But even the most placid lapdog is descended from canine predators, so all dog owners need to be watchful and develop strategies for handling the occasional problems that
do crop up.

Pal or Predator?

All dogs have a dual nature. On one side is the gentle, eager-to-please companion. On the other is the pack hunter descended from canines that preyed on other animals for food.

Dogs have all the necessary sensory and physical "equipment" to detect and chase small (and sometimes not-so-small) animals. Moving objects tend to set off a dog's chasing impulse. So you may see your otherwise placid pet take off after fleeing animals—be they squirrels or another family pet. "The impulse to chase can be so overwhelming that even a very obedient dog may disregard commands," says Dr. Bruce Fogle, a London-based veterinarian and author. And predatory behavior is self-reinforcing if a dog regularly succeeds in capturing its "prey."

Over the centuries, humans have honed canine predatory skills through selective breeding. For example, people bred sighthounds, such as greyhounds and Afghan hounds, to pursue prey, and many of today's terrier breeds are descended from dogs that were valued mainly in terms of their rodent-killing abilities. Herding, one of the most time-honored canine professions, is actually a modified form of predation. Even the pouncing and stalking of a dog's play behavior is a whimsical variation of predation. When we try to discourage dogs from instinctive predatory behavior, we are, contends Dr. Dodman, "swimming against the genetic tide."

Speaking "Dogese"

When two species confront each other for the first time, each wonders which is dominant over (or predatory toward) the other. But the body-language "vocabulary" of different species is different. Two dogs meeting for the first time figure out who's who and what's what by sniffing, standing, and moving in certain mutually understood ways. But when cats and other animals that don't speak "dogese" meet a dog for the first time, they are often frightened. For example, any dog socialized with its own kind knows that a play bow—front legs

and torso down, rear end up—is an invitation to frolic. But to a cat, this posture may seem threatening—or at the very least, perplexing. Instead of offering a friendly response to the classic play bow, Felix may scrunch up into the "Halloween pose," with back arched, tail puffed, and a grimacing hiss. The playful dog—misreading the cat's message—may venture forward and wind up with a clawed snout.

The Right Foundation

The best chance for tranquility in a multispecies household comes from planning. Both Drs. Dodman and Fogle stress the importance of early cross-species exposure and proper training. "Early experience is by far the most important factor in shaping how dogs and other animals live together as adults," says Dr. Fogle. The ideal scenario is when two young animals grow up together.

Although introducing young animals is usually better, many pet owners have had success introducing already mature animals into homes with dogs. If you are planning to do this, reinforce your dog's basic obedience training before bringing in the new animal. A dog that sits, stays, and comes in the presence of another animal is going to have an easier time adapting to a new companion than one without this training.

Sometimes species just don't mix. If the incumbent dog or cat is an old curmudgeon, respect its seniority and don't bring home a new animal. Also, the breed of dog may be at least as important as age and temperament in determining how well two species get along. If your next-door neighbor raises sheep, for example, think twice about selecting a border collie as your family dog. And terriers, observes Dr. Fogle, are more likely than some other breeds to be aggressive toward cats.

Proper Introductions

Once you've laid the groundwork for an interspecies relationship, give some thought to first introductions. Your main goal is to minimize conflict by gradually exposing the animals to one another. "Don't plop the cat in front of the dog and say, 'Sylvester, this is your new friend Rover,'" cautions Dr. Fogle.

The ideal venue for a first meeting is neutral outdoor territory. But since bringing a dog and a cat to the park on leashes isn't usually practical, an indoor introduction may be your only option. In indoor situations, it's best to restrict the newcomer's range and keep the animals in separate areas for several days. But it's easier to do this if the new family member is a cat; felines tolerate restricted spaces better than most dogs.

Before a face-to-face meeting, let your animals check each other out through a door that's opened just wide enough for them to smell—but not touch—one another. "Watch carefully for any negative reaction in either animal," advises Dr. Dodman. (If the dog whines incessantly when the cat is nearby, the dog may have predatory interests.) Also, feed the animals on opposite sides of the partition—close but not too close—so they begin to associate pleasure with being near each other.

Despite your best efforts, the first meeting (and later interactions) between two animals of different species may still pose some danger to them. More than one dog has had its eyes or nose scratched by a confused or frightened feline, and dogs can inflict even greater harm on cats. So the safest whisker-to-whisker meetings are always those supervised by owners.

No Guarantees

Despite interspecies language barriers, most dogs readily accept non-dogs—including humans and other household pets—as members of their pack. But Bowser may not display the same level of acceptance toward "outsider" cats as he does toward cats he lives with. Says Dr. Dodman, "A dog raised with a cat usually won't chase that cat, but the same dog might chase other cats."

Even when dogs and other animals live in peace most of the time, occasional flare-ups may occur. And pack behavior—the same behavior that promotes sociability—may also promote conflict. "There is always the potential for a group of dogs to gang up on another animal," says Dr. Fogle.

Negotiating a Truce

Sometimes, domestic relationships among pets get off on the wrong paw, and owners must become referees. Outdoors, dogs may harass other animals that stray within their territory, including neighborhood kitties. Both indoors and outdoors, these problems can usually be resolved.

■ *Try obedience training first. A basic refresher course for your dog should include at least four commands: "sit," "come," "stay," and "no" (or "leave it").*

■ *Desensitization may also help, but this time-consuming process requires oodles of patience. During desensitization, you train your dog to stay calm in the presence of another animal by very gradually exposing it to the other species. You start the process by positioning the animals at a great distance from one another and exposing them to each other for short periods of time. Over a number of weeks, gradually bring the animals closer together. Always reward the dog for peaceful, benign behavior.*

■ *Medication may help. If your dog is too wound up for obedience training or desensitization, ask your veterinarian about medication. Recent evidence suggests that certain psychoactive drugs borrowed from human medicine may help calm dogs so effective training becomes possible. If your dog presents a real danger to another animal, consider using a properly fitted basket muzzle during training. (For the long term, though, muzzling is not the answer.)*

There are rare cases where two animals—either housemates or neighbors—simply don't get along. If your repeated conciliatory efforts prove unsuccessful, you may find the only practical solution is enforced separation. If the combatants happen to be cohabitants, find a loving, single-pet home for one of the animals. If neighboring animals are in conflict, you'll have to do whatever is necessary to avoid confrontations.

Best of Friends

Notwithstanding the occasional hiss or snarl, peaceful cohabitation is the norm for dogs living with other animals. Although animals speak different languages, owners can—with a little preparation, effort, and patience—promote harmony in a multispecies, "multilingual" household. ❧

11

Getting Along:
The Language of Peace

Interpret and foster canines' instinctive use of
"calming signals" to send messages of
non-aggression and cooperation.

During the early morning hours, the lions brought down a large giraffe. Enjoying their good fortune, the several lionesses, their cubs and the two handsome males ate their fill. As the day advanced and the heat became oppressive, they stretched out in the shade keeping a watchful eye on the remains of their meal.

Nearby, a jackal, cousin to the wolf and the domestic dog, sat patiently eyeing the pride and the carcass, hoping for a snack. The jackal looked at the lions, then turned his head and looked away. Again he looked back and this time he yawned.

Was the jackal merely tired from waiting? No, he was using calming signals, the universal canine language of peace, to avoid raising the ire of the lions. The wild canids of Africa and our companion dogs here at home share the same complex language of gesture designed to keep things mellow. In the turn of a head, the blink of an eye, a lick of the nose or a yawn, a whole story unfolds in the canine lexicon.

Turid Rugaas, an inquisitive Norwegian dog trainer and patient observer of canine behavior, has identified 27 different gestures dogs use to communicate with each other, signs she has labeled calming signals. Dogs and other canines use such signals to send messages of non-aggression to other dogs and animals of all species including us. The calming signals are thought to help relax the communicators themselves, at the same time.

Focus on Getting Along

The earliest wolf researchers focused largely on the aggressive tendencies in their subjects. Terms like "alpha female" and "dominance and submission" quickly entered our vocabulary when speaking about the behavior of dogs. Those researchers also spoke of cut-off signals in wolves, body language designed to cut off signs of aggression. But Rugaas says calming signals do more than stop aggression; they are proactive communications to help foster cooperation.

Rugaas acknowledges that wolves are a communal species. They live in packs and therefore must have a complex language and social structure designed to foster group dynamics. Think of the skills we must develop to get along with just a single partner, never mind a complex extended family.

For wolves, the pack is necessary for survival. Food is essential and so is the hunt. To bring down a large prey animal takes tremendous cooperation among pack members. Developing and maintaining a language to keep the peace is as essential for wolf survival as is getting the next meal. Wolves and dogs have a strong instinct for conflict solving, communication and cooperation, all a necessary

This young black Lab is extremely skilled at "explaining" how friendly and unthreatening he is. He stands still, not facing the Shepherd cross.

Rolling over on his back is a classic submissive gesture, but combined with the lick of the nose, he signals more than just submission: he wants to be friends.

part of pack behavior. They instinctively know they must get along in order to survive.

Our domestic dogs share much of the same DNA as wolves. According to Rugaas, the most frightening thing for a dog is to be alone. While we can teach them to accept aloneness, we must remember that by nature they, too, need a pack to feel safe. Without other dogs in the home, we become their pack. Learning their language can foster maximum respect and cooperation; when in Rome, speak Italian!

How Dogs Learn the Language

Pups who are raised in a litter for the first eight weeks of their lives (and in the presence of older dogs) have the advantage of learning skills from their siblings and elders. They learn to accept the leadership of a just leader. They learn simple, but crucially important lessons such as bite inhibition. They come to understand when play is too rough or inappropriate. And they have the opportunity to learn the language skills that will enable them to be peaceful pack members.

According to Rugaas, dogs inherited the calming signals from their wolf forbears. All the different breeds all over the world – no matter what size, color, or shape they are – display these signals. "It is a truly universal language and a wonderful one because it means we can communicate with dogs wherever we meet them," says Rugaas.

"Canine language in general consists of a large variety of signals using body, face, ears, tail, sounds, movement, and expression. The dogs' innate ability to signal is easily lost or reinforced through life's experience," she says. "When we remove pups from their litters too early, or when we keep them from other dogs, even to prevent early puppyhood diseases, we may be doing them a great disservice by depriving them of the chance to practice their own language."

SPARKY HAS JUST MADE FIVE ATTEMPTS TO CALM YOU DOWN: SNIFFING, TURNING HIS HEAD, LICKING HIS NOSE, ADVANCING IN A CURVED LINE, AND MOVING SLOWLY.

Dogs Often Try To Calm *US*

The most obvious signals used by dogs are the threat signals: Barking, hardening the eyes, and showing teeth are fairly easy to notice. Charging and snapping gets anyone's attention. Biting is pretty tough to miss. But we usually overlook the equally important calming signals. Our dogs are always trying to communicate with us, but are we listening, or should I say looking?

Say you have come home late from work, frustrated that you have to go out again to a meeting. Or maybe you just want to catch a movie to relax, but you only have 20 minutes to change clothes and leave again! You greet Sparky at the door. He, of course, showers you with affection and enthusiasm by jumping in your face, while telling you vocally how happy he is to see you. You let him out in the yard to do his business. He runs this way and that, checking up on the news of the day by sniffing the lawn and bushes. When he is done relieving himself, you call him to come in. You've checked your watch and you are now running late. There is a bit of urgency in your voice. "Sparky, come!"

But Sparky starts sniffing again, and annoyed, you call him once more. This time Sparky looks up at you, then turns his head to the side, licks his nose and starts coming toward the back door in what appears to be a roundabout way, a curved route if you ever saw one. And he slows down. You may be sure he's just trying to make you late, but you are mistaken. Sparky has just made five attempts to calm you down: sniffing, turning his head, licking his nose, advancing in a curved line, and moving slowly. He has heard your irritation and knows something is amiss. He's offering his best attempt to help you stay cool.

Let's look at a few of the calming signals below and expand our "vocabulary."

■ Sniffing

Of course, dogs sniff to sniff smells. But your dog may do it when another dog is approaching her, when someone is walking straight at her, or when a sudden situation occurs – for instance two dogs are suddenly too close. Or if you call your dog to you in a harsh voice or from a full front position. Face-to-face, eye-to-eye posture to a dog can be construed as somewhat aggressive or dangerous, so some calming down may be in order.

A very dog-aggressive Rottweiler I once worked with would root like a pig, sniffing furiously, when she first saw a dog approaching from a distance. Without understanding her need to send a calming message to the intruder, her owner, tugging on the leash, would deprive the dog of her "peace-maker's voice." Fearful of other dogs, the Rottie would then lunge like a barking fury to tell the perceived adversary to stay away.

■ Turning the head

All signals may be quick movements or, as here, the head can be held to the side for some time. It may be as small as a looking away of the eyes or may involve turning the whole body away.

Your dog may turn her head to the side when a stranger approaches or a child offers an inappropriate hug. When two dogs meet, they may both look away for a second, and then greet each other happily. A self-assured dog may approach your dog very directly, but averting his eyes from side to side, sending the message that he is a friendly fellow. Your dog may lick her nose, turn her head to the side and be ready for a big hello.

This is a signal we can use to help greet scared, shy, or aggressive-behaving dogs. By approaching a new dog at an oblique angle and looking away, we can send the message that we are friend, not foe.

■ Licking the nose

This can be a very quick movement of the tongue that is difficult to see, or it may be a clean swipe of the nose. Your dog may use it when being approached by another dog, or when you bend over your dog or make him uncomfortable in some way. Black dogs, whose facial features are not as easy to see from a distance, may use the licking signal more often.

Rugaas says it is a difficult one for people to use, but I use it having assumed that by licking my lips, though not actually getting to my nose, I'm "speaking" an understandable dialect.

■ Yawning

This is a signal easily used by humans. It was the one chosen by our jackal to speak to lions. Your dog may yawn when at the veterinarian's office or when being approached by a stranger. You may use it when your dog is a bit stressed, worried, scared, or when you want him to calm down. I have watched dogs look up at me in apparent amazement when they see me yawn and realize I am speaking their language.

Other signals include walking slowly or using slow movements, sitting down, lying down or using a stretch-in-place or the play bow. Walking in a curved line, lifting the paw, twirling around each other and blinking the eyes are also calming signals.

BY SHARPENING OUR POWERS OF OBSERVATION, WE CAN BEGIN OUR OWN ADVENTURE OF EXPLORATION WITH OUR CANINE COMPANIONS AND ASSIST THEM AT THE SAME TIME.

Teaching the Signals to Dogs

Rugaas employs her knowledge of these signals when introducing two dog-aggressive or shy dogs. With each dog on leash, she has their handlers approach from a distance allowing each animal to sniff, look away, lick or yawn as it chooses. By monitoring their reactions, she orchestrates the meeting, keeping the anxiety level low.

She does the same when introducing a shy dog to a new person. She may have the person approach in a curve, walking slowly, looking away and even sitting on the ground. By gauging the dog's reaction she knows when it's safe to let the dog come over to greet the person. Sometimes it may take more than one session.

By sharpening our powers of observation, we can begin our own adventure of exploration with our canine companions and assist them at the same time.

Boosting Interspecies Communication

I recently helped introduce a cat and dog who had to share a new house with each other. The cat was very self-assured and knew how to hold her own. The dog had lived and even slept with a cat before. The dog had great communication skills. My role became that of mediator. We handled the introductions slowly, observing the dialogue that took place between our two charges.

The cat was placed on the people bed in the dog's room, while the dog was out of sight on the porch. As Elise, the cat, became comfortable, we brought Tucker, the dog, to the glass door. He cautiously looked away and licked his nose. The cat took the opportunity to study the dog, then she looked away, blinking her eyes. The dog now looked at the cat and looked away again.

Next, we brought Tucker into the room at a distance, and the dialogue continued. As they seemed to get more comfortable with each other, the dog yawned, then looked away once more. If Tucker looked a little too long at Elise, I called his name getting him to look at me and away from her. I had him sit, lie down and come to me, offering him food treats as incentive and reward, giving Elise the chance to see him in action.

By the end of the hour session, Tucker and Elise had both had a chance to observe each other in close proximity while feeling safe. The cat's person had petted the dog, and the dog's person had held the cat on his lap. The animals could see that each wanted to cooperate. We ended by allowing Elise to leave in her own good time. She hopped off the bed looking away from Tucker and slowly walked out the open door. Outside she licked herself, apparently pleased by the outcome. Tucker was equally happy and relaxed.

The next time you go to the dog park bring along your understanding of calming signals and check out the action. As you sharpen your observation skills, a whole new world will open before your eyes, and soon you, too, can get on talking terms with dogs. And while you're at it, pay attention to your response when people make eye contact with you. Do you avert your eyes, walk across the street or flicker a brief smile? Maybe you already know more about calming signals than you think. ❧

Section III

Early Learning

12

Ain't Misbehavin'

*Work with a dog's instincts to modify
his behavior into something positive—and create an
incredibly rewarding bond between the two of you.*

Not far below the furry surface of your favorite domestic canine companion lurks a mind surprisingly similar to that of its ancestor and current-day cousin, the wolf. We have stretched and molded the dog's plastic genetic material to create hundreds of widely diverse breeds – from the tiny Chihuahua to the giant St. Bernard – all to serve our whims. But our dogs' behaviors and instincts to this day closely mirror those chosen by natural selection to ensure the wolf's survival some 10,000 to 15,000 years ago, when the wild canine was first invited to share the warmth and protection of the fires in our ancestors' caves.

The genetics that have enabled the dog to become "man's best friend" come as both a blessing and a curse. The instincts that drive the behaviors we love in our canine companions are the same ones that make us tear our hair out. For example, the desire to be a member of a social group, or pack, is what makes the dog so amenable to family life and training. It is this same social instinct that in some dogs triggers incredibly destructive "separation anxiety" behaviors when a dog is left alone, behaviors that include non-stop barking and howling, inappropriate urination and defecation, chewing, and self-destructive escape attempts.

When their behaviors and instincts are understood and properly directed, our dogs are well-adjusted, cherished family members. The millions of dogs that are abandoned at animal shelters in the U.S. every year are tragic testimony to how often we fail to do this.

Let's look at how we can prevent this from happening to your dog.

Dog trainers commonly hear complaints about dogs that bite, attack other dogs, jump up, bark, chase cats, cars, or joggers, are shy, or don't come when called. All these activities have a basis in normal, instinctive, survival-based canine behavior. They occur in spite of the owner's training efforts because the dog is rewarded by them in some way.

Fortunately, each behavior can be modified, either by figuring out how to make the desired behavior more rewarding than the undesirable one, or by managing the dog so he doesn't have an opportunity to exhibit the inappropriate behavior. Traditional training methods have often relied on human logic to teach dogs how to behave, by punishing the dog for "bad" behavior. But in the minds of our dogs, behavior is neither good nor bad; they are just doing what dogs do, driven by instinct and governed by the consequences of their actions. "Good" behavior is learned behavior. They learn more quickly, effectively, and happily if we focus on rewarding the "right" behaviors, and preventing, or to the extent possible, ignoring, the "wrong" ones.

Start When They Are Young

Early management and training is the best approach, since it's easier to prevent an undesirable behavior than it is to correct it. For this reason, more and more dog trainers offer classes for puppies as young as 10 weeks. Trainers used to recommend waiting until a dog was six months old to start training classes, in part because of the widespread use of "choke chains," which can damage the soft cartilage of a puppy's throat. Now that positive-based training is more widely accepted and available (using a standard flat buckle collar or head collar, and rewards and praise instead of leash-jerk corrections), there is no reason to wait. Owners can take advantage of a puppy's critical socialization period to teach good behaviors.

The socialization period is a time when puppies in the wild have to learn quickly in order to survive. During the same critical period, domestic puppies learn which behaviors are acceptable to their human pack, which are rewarding, and which things are safe. While some veterinarians still counsel keeping a dog isolated at home until it is fully vaccinated by age four to six months, enlightened animal-care professionals recognize that there is far greater risk to our dogs' lives (through euthanasia at an animal shelter) if they do not learn to be well-socialized and well-behaved during this critical learning period. Many veterinarians now strongly encourage their clients to pursue puppy classes and other controlled socializing activities as long as the pups have received at least two vaccinations and the owner keeps up with the necessary schedule of puppy shots.

The Shrinking Violet

Shyness can be genetic, it can result from lack of socialization, or it can be a combination of the two. While the wolf puppy that takes a "no fear" attitude doesn't live long, neither does a wild pup who is so afraid of his own shadow that he doesn't leave the den long enough to find adequate food to eat. Reasoned caution is a good survival skill for all dogs, wild and domestic. But because domestic dogs don't face the life-threatening forces that wild ones do, genetically shy dogs can and do survive to reproduce, especially when assisted by irresponsible breeders and puppy mills.

While all puppies need to be properly socialized (even the bold ones), it is even more imperative to socialize the shy puppy. Left to his own devices, his timid behavior will intensify and he will grow up to be fearful, neurotic, and dangerous.

With these little guys, the flight response is so strong that it is important to be patient. Let the pup initiate contact with strange people or objects and reward each contact with a tasty treat (see page 10 for treat suggestions). Don't force the pup. Forced contact will aggravate the fear/flight response and make the shyness worse. But don't coddle him, either. Coddling rewards and encourages fear behavior. Be gentle, patient, matter-of-fact, and upbeat about helping him understand and accept the big, scary world.

Come Again?

Puppies, wild or domestic, naturally stay close to other pack members. Again, it's a survival thing; the puppy that wanders away ends up as hawk food. Our eight-week-old puppies usually come running when we call them because they are very dependent and want to be near us more than anything else in the world. We soon believe that they have learned to come when we call them. When they get older and more independent, and start to explore the world on their own, they no longer come when we call. We are convinced that they are being stubborn, ignoring us on purpose.

In fact, they never learned to come when called. Now, if they get reprimanded when they do come back (for not coming when they were called) they are even less likely to come the next time they are called, since they have learned that the consequence for coming is punishment, not reward.

In order to teach a reliable "come," we capitalize on the dog's desire to be near us and the instinct to seek rewards. When your pup is a baby and comes to you easily, be sure to reward with treats and praise every time. Never punish "come!" If you have to correct for something (like getting in the garbage), don't call her – go to the pup to administer the mild correction. If she doesn't come to you when you need her to, resist the urge to chase after her. She'll think "chase the dog" is a wonderful game. Instead, turn and run away, doing something to get her attention – like making excited, high-pitched noises, squeaking a squeaky toy, or bouncing a ball. Teaching her to "chase" you engages her prey drive and takes advantage of her instinct to stay with the pack (you) and her strong desire to be a part of exciting pack activities.

THE MAJORITY OF BITES TO HUMANS
OCCUR BECAUSE WE MISREAD OR IGNORE
THE DOG'S WARNING SIGNS.

Taking The Bite Out

Of all unwanted behaviors, biting is the least socially acceptable to humans, and the one that most often results in a death sentence for the dog. Yet biting is a totally natural behavior for dogs, both wild and domestic. Wolf puppies and adults bite each other in play and in warning. Very rarely do they bite each other in order to do serious damage. It is vital to the survival of the pack that all members be strong and healthy. It makes no sense for pack members to engage in fierce battles that might result in serious injury. As pups, they learn the importance of bite inhibition by playing with each other. When a pup bites a littermate too hard, the victim yelps loudly and may refuse to play for a while. Thus the biter learns that the fun of play ends when he bites too hard. Over the first five months of his life, he learns to control the strength of his bite. If he doesn't have this opportunity, it is much more difficult for him to learn to use his mouth gently later.

Enter the human. We routinely take the domestic puppy away from his siblings at six to eight weeks, sometimes earlier, effectively eliminating the pup's opportunity to learn bite inhibition. No wonder we end up with shark-puppies who chomp down on our hands, sometimes even drawing blood with their needle-sharp teeth!

Responsible breeders won't release their puppies to new homes until they are at least eight, sometimes ten weeks of age or older. Progressive animal shelters put litters of young pups in foster homes so they can grow and learn from each other, rather than placing them too early. Yet, trusting in the myth that "the earlier you get a pup the more she will bond with you," uneducated dog owners clamor for the six-week-old puppy (or younger). Unethical breeders, uneducated backyard breeders and shelters that lack adequate foster programs may oblige.

Even if adopted at eight to ten weeks, pups need to continue their bite inhibition lessons. The best way for the human teacher to do this is to imitate the puppy's littermates. When a pup bites hard, say "OUCH!" in a loud, high-pitched squeak and remove yourself from the pup's reach for a few minutes. Then return to puppy play. Each time the pup bites too hard, repeat the lesson.

After several repetitions the pup's bite will begin to soften. You can then repeat the lesson at gradually decreasing levels of bite intensity until the pup learns not to bite at all. If you try to extinguish bite behavior all at once you will frustrate your puppy's natural biting behavior, and fail at the task. At the same time you are softening the bite you can also direct the puppy's biting toward acceptable chew items. (It is virtually impossible for small children to respond properly and consistently to puppy biting, which is why many shelters and responsible breeders discourage families with young children from adopting young puppies.)

Adult dog biting behavior is much more serious. Much of wolf body language is designed to avoid an actual fight, again for individual and pack survival reasons. Growls, stiffened legs, stiffly wagging tails, stares, glares, and raised hackles are signals intended to warn away a challenger. The majority of bites to humans occur because we misread or ignore the dog's similar warning signs. This is one reason why children are so often the victim of dog bites – they are even less skilled than adults at heeding a dog's warning – and why it is so important for adults to supervise all interactions between dogs and small children, no matter how trustworthy the dog is believed to be.

A wolf or dog's reaction to a possible threat is either to stand ground and fight, or flee. Individual canines usually have a preference for one reaction style over the other. Most dogs that prefer to stand and fight will still give warnings. If they are ignored, a bite often follows. We call this "dominance aggression." A dog who prefers flight will try to escape the threat rather than challenge it, but if the escape route is cut off – when a dog is cornered, restrained, or tied up – a bite often follows. We call this submission aggression, or "fear biting."

The more a puppy is socialized before the age of five months, the fewer things are ultimately perceived as threatening, and the less likely it is that a bite will occur in the adult dog.

Jump Back, Jack!

All creatures instinctively seek rewards. In order to take advantage of instinct-driven behaviors, we just need to figure out how to make the behavior we want more rewarding than the one we don't want, and then continue to reinforce the "right" behavior until it is a programmed response.

Wolves, of course, don't have much opportunity to jump up on people. They do greet each other face-to-face – sniffing noses and licking faces. Our dogs jump on us in their greeting ritual to try to reach our faces (and will often lick our faces if we let them), to demand attention, and because when they are puppies we pick them up and cuddle them, teaching them that "up" is a very rewarding place to be.

When they jump up they are self-rewarded simply by touching us. Everything we do to get them off of us also rewards them. We look at them. Eye contact is a reward. We push them away. We touched them – that's a reward! We tell them to get off. We spoke to them – that's a reward too! A sturdy, rambunctious dog can view even a forceful "knee in the chest" as an invitation to play.

If, instead, we ignore the behavior we don't want (in this case by turning away from the dog, and stepping away so he isn't even self-rewarded by touching us) and reward the behavior we do want (by waiting or asking for the dog to sit, then turning to him, and giving him a treat, along with the greeting and attention he wants) he will soon learn that he gets rewarding by running up to us and sitting, rather than jumping.

The Thrill of the Chase

The wolf would not survive without a strong prey drive. The lives of pack members depend on their ability to chase, catch and kill things that run away from them. Our dogs have retained a very strong prey drive. In many cases, we use this instinctive behavior to our advantage. The intense herding behavior of the Border Collie is a modified prey drive with a strong inhibition for the killing part of the process. Many breeds of terriers, hounds, and sporting dogs were bred to pursue and kill or retrieve other animals. We encourage this drive in our pets to this day, with mutually enjoyable games of fetch the Frisbee, stick, dumbbell, and tennis ball.

Small wonder, then, that some dogs are driven to chase cats, joggers, bicycles, cars, and other fast-moving objects. This is such a strong drive in some dogs that it is difficult, if not impossible, to eliminate. Prevention is mandatory for your dog's own safety. Dogs who are allowed to run loose to chase cars tend to have short lives. Dogs who chase cats, joggers and kids soon get in trouble with neighbors and animal control. Dogs who chase livestock get shot. With a real commitment to a long-term training program we can teach our dogs to pay attention and respond to us even in the presence of an enticing prey-distraction, but a dog with a strong prey-drive will always chase if given the opportunity, and must always be securely confined when not under the owner's immediate control.

Hark, a Bark

Barking is also a natural behavior. In fact, when Lassie barks to warn us of an intruder, or to tell us that Timmy has fallen in the well, she's a hero. But if she barks at the mail carrier, a stray cat in the yard, or when Aunt Emma knocks on the front door, we yell at her to "Shut up!" It is a wolf's job to alert other members of the pack to anything out of the ordinary, and when Lassie barks at the mail carrier, she's just doing her job. How is she supposed to know when we want her to alert us and when we don't? Some dogs may well think that "Shut up" is just our way of joining in the barking! A better way to respond is to acknowledge the intruder and thank Lassie for doing her job. Then tell her that you have everything under control, with a "Good girl, that's all, quiet." Again, with a positive-reward approach, you wait for the barking to stop, and reward the silence with a treat while you say "Good dog, quiet."

A dog who barks non-stop in the backyard is a different matter. Non-stop barking is often a sign of a dog who is bored and lonely. She is isolated from her human pack and expressing her natural desire to rejoin the social order. The obvious solution is to bring the dog into the house and let her be part of the pack. Crate-training (teaching the dog to sleep in a wire kennel or airline crate) is an excellent tool to help incorporate the dog into the family without risking damage to antique furniture and Oriental carpets. Dogs are meant to live with others – isolating a dog is a form of extreme mental cruelty, and should not be permitted.

THE NEXT TIME YOUR DOG DOES SOMETHING YOU DON'T LIKE, STOP AND THINK BEFORE YOU YELL. HE'S NOT BEING BAD – HE'S BEING A DOG.

Endless Possibilities

Most dog behaviors are connected in some way to that genetic package of instincts handed down from the wolf. And all dog behavior, if properly managed, can be turned into something positive. Dogs that dig can find truffles in France. Dogs that climb and jump fences are great candidates for agility training. The hound that always runs off with his nose to the ground can learn to track and do Search and Rescue. Dogs that chase can fetch golf balls. Their potential is limited only by our creativity.

The next time your dog does something you don't like, stop and think before you yell. He's not being bad – he's being a dog. What instinct is driving his behavior? How can you work with his instincts instead of against them to modify his behavior into something positive? It's worth the time it takes to figure it out and apply it to his training. You'll end up with a happier dog. You'll be a much happier dog owner. The incredibly rewarding bond that is created between the two of you will guarantee that your dog never ends up in the ranks of the homeless hounds at your local humane society. ❧

13

Let's Play!

*Play teaches puppies physical and social skills,
including "adaptive flexibility"—the ability
to adjust to life's stresses.*

A s Janet takes a stroll with her puppy Coco, another dog
approaches with movements that are more balletic than
aggressive. The dog skids sideways, lowers its front end,
and sticks its tail-wagging rear high in the air. The dog's
message is unmistakable: "Coco, let's play!"

Play's Purpose

The exaggerated, often comical antics of our dogs at play seem to
give them pure pleasure. But wild animals also expend energy and
sometimes risk injury to play, suggesting that play has a practical
purpose as well.

And indeed it does. Play teaches puppies both physical and social skills. At a mere 3 weeks of age, puppies begin to bite and paw
playfully at each other. When a pup bites too hard, the victim's yelps
teach the aggressor to back off. This bite inhibition is an impulse
control most owners are grateful for.

By 4 to 5 weeks, most pups have learned several signals to solicit play, and their rascally play repertoire has become more varied.
Chasing, pouncing, scruff-shaking, and wrestling all increase puppies' strength and coordination and teach them how to communicate their dominance or submission—the building blocks of canine
social organization. Also at 4 to 5 weeks, puppies start vocalizing

during play—emitting low-pitched growls and snarls; sharp, repetitive "yips"; and long, plaintive howls.

At 5 to 6 weeks, a major part of puppy play is exploration, which educates the puppy about its environment. (That newspaper doesn't taste good, some floors are slippery and cold, stairs are steep.) Play also teaches pups important problem-solving skills, such as how to escape from a pen and how to extract a toy from a tight spot. At this stage, pups also engage in playful pseudosexual behavior such as mounting—practicing for adulthood.

Over time, play instills in dogs what behaviorists call adaptive flexibility—the ability to adjust to life's stresses (such as a change in owners, a period of intensive training, or hospitalization). But due to abuse, neglect, or premature separation from littermates, some dogs don't learn to play as pups. Consequently, they fail to develop adaptive skills and may grow into canine introverts—fearful of people, other dogs, noises, and sudden movement. "Through carefully controlled play with humans and other dogs, the social skills of these dogs can be significantly improved, although most retain some residual deficits," says Dr. Bruce Fogle, a London-based veterinarian and author.

Picking Your Breed

Playfulness is one characteristic to consider when choosing a breed. Some of the more independent breeds such as basset hounds and basenjis are genetically programmed to be less playful than dogs bred to work closely with humans, such as retrievers and herding dogs.

Beyond Puppy Play

Although they play less frequently than puppies, "adult dogs use play to establish and confirm their social status, to maintain strength and coordination, and to facilitate courtship," says Dr. Jean DeNapoli, a resident at the Behavior Clinic at Tufts University School of Veterinary Medicine. Solitary play with inanimate objects provides intellectual stimulation and hones problem-solving skills. Interestingly, older dogs secure in their social standing may play more often than they did as young adults. For most dogs, play is an important way to exercise and a source of intellectual stimulation well into old age.

Training Tool

Most dog trainers agree that play can be a versatile training tool. When used as a positive reinforcer (a reward for desirable behavior), play accelerates the learning process. And "time out" for play can relieve the stress of an intense training session.

In addition, you can use games to teach dogs specific exercises. For example, you can teach a dog with no burning desire to retrieve how to fetch via play. To awaken Bowser's "chase" instinct, attach a string to the object you want him to retrieve and twitch it a little before you throw it. Run away as soon as he picks up the object; his "following" instinct should kick in. Voilà—the retrieve!

Hunting Games

Many of the games dogs invent on their own derive from instinctive hunting behavior. A windblown leaf skittering across the ground becomes a scampering mouse; a fluttering plastic bag becomes fleeing skin and fur. The squeaky and fleecy chew toys we provide also simulate prey. And hollow objects, such as rubber Kong® toys stuffed with treats and sealed with peanut butter, resemble the bones of prey animals full of delectable, extractable marrow.

Playmates and Soulmates

Animals play most often with others of their own kind, but they also cavort with other species. Nature photographers have captured dogs playing with polar bears (a natural canine predator), and we often see dogs playing with cats.

Since both dogs and humans play with their own species to build relationships, it's not surprising that play also has a powerful role in cementing the human-canine bond. When playing, participants drop their inhibitions and have a chance to interact in spontaneous, nonthreatening ways. Because play reduces stress and restores energy, it's probably the best way to spend time with your dog. Next time your dog "asks" you to play, how can you refuse?

Open Invitations

Most people are familiar with the canine play bow —the head-down, tail-up position that invites play. But dogs also solicit play with a "play face"—ears erect and lips pulled back in a sort of grin.

Here are some interactive games that are both aerobic and mentally stimulating for dogs and their people:

■ Fetch
Whether it's a ball or a disc, dogs love to chase and catch moving objects. Throw low to prevent injury from airborne jumps and twists.

■ Chase
Grab your dog's favorite toy and run with it. Then let your dog reclaim the toy and run. This "role reversal" game can build confidence in shy dogs, but overexcited dogs may start to jump around uncontrollably. If this happens, put your dog in a sit-stay until it calms down.

■ Soccer
Using your feet, maintain control of a large ball made of resilient but puncture-proof plastic. Let your canine friend have possession at least half the time. (This game may not be suitable for chronic heel nippers.)

■ Hide-and-Seek:
Show Bowser his favorite toy; then put him in a sit-stay while you hide it. After you release him, encourage him as he gets closer to the hidden object; remain silent when he moves in the wrong direction. Hiding yourself makes for an interesting variation.

■ Tug-of-War
Although this game is a perennial favorite, you should play it only with a dog that will stop immediately on command. This type of play can escalate into aggression, especially with dominant dogs. Never play tug-of-war with a dog that has shown aggression toward people. ❧

14

Blissful Obedience

*During a puppy's critical learning and
socialization period, from 4 to 12 weeks of age, you
can readily teach it to sit and come.*

Cleo is poised to romp across the street to greet Fred, her canine chum. "Cleo, come!" commands Cleo's owner, Beverly. Ears up, tail wagging, Cleo turns on a dime and bounds back to Beverly. A second later, a speeding car whizzes by. "What a good girl!"

As duos like Cleo and Beverly know, teaming up to learn basic obedience commands has important practical value. Aside from potentially prolonging your dog's life, obedience training strengthens the natural bond between you and your dog.

Although "basic obedience" may sound dull, training can be enjoyable. The mainstays of training—praise, play, petting (and anything else you and your dog enjoy)—make learning fun.

When to Start

Basic obedience should begin as soon as you get your dog. Puppies as young as 7 or 8 weeks old are trainable. During a puppy's critical learning and socialization period (from 4 to 12 weeks), you can readily teach it to sit and come. Those who wait until their dogs are 5 months old (the youngest age at which most formal obedience schools accept students) are at a disadvantage—because after a puppy's first 3 months, its learning rate slows down. Old dogs *can* learn new tricks, however, so it's never too late to start.

Puppy training is most successful when you do it in a quiet area free from distractions. Once your pup understands a few simple commands, you should continue training in the midst of background noise, other dogs, or people. Socializing your pup at the same time you train it will boost its confidence and emotional stability—and accelerate learning. "It's just as important to socialize your dog as it is to train it," says Dr. Nicholas Dodman, director of the Behavior Clinic at Tufts University School of Veterinary Medicine.

As your dog enters adolescence (9 to 24 months), it may challenge your authority. If you don't consistently assert your leadership, your dog may assume the role because dogs expect every "pack" to have a leader. This is not canine mutiny. Your dog is simply acting on its instinctive need for someone to take charge and be "top dog."

Many of us acquire adult dogs from shelters or rescue organizations. Immediate (and continuing) work in basic obedience helps these dogs and their owners establish and maintain mutually respectful, cooperative relationships. (As mentioned previously, however, dogs older than 12 weeks may not learn as quickly or as permanently as they would have if trained earlier.)

Think Like a Dog

Whether you work with your dog on your own or enlist the help of a dog trainer or animal behaviorist, the most challenging aspect of basic obedience is helping your dog understand what you want it to do. Most approaches to obedience training (and there are many!) focus on training you to think like your dog.

Even though dogs sometimes seem to outsmart humans, their mental processes are not as complex as ours. Dogs are easily confused by mixed or ambiguous messages. For example, many novices repeat commands until their dogs finally perform the desired behavior and then wonder later why the dog won't respond immediately. You must insist on obedience the first time and enthusiastically praise your dog.

Dogs also get confused when they come on command and receive a reprimand (often for an earlier transgression). A dog in this situation probably thinks, "I obeyed, I came, I got punished." Don't expect Caesar to come on command again after that kind of treatment. Remember, disobedient dogs are not spiteful; they simply misunderstand what their owners want.

When training your dog, keep things simple. Training commands must be short and unambiguous. "Communicating with a dog in sentences doesn't work," observes Dr. Dodman. (For example, "Sit!" is more effective than "Can you sit for me?") In addition, dogs respond more readily to consistent tone of voice than to meaning. You should deliver commands with a calm but authoritative voice. Deliver praise with a gleeful, higher-pitched tone, and give reprimands with a low, gruff tone. Dogs are also astute observers of body language, so use hand signals to help your dog understand your verbal commands.

Because mental concentration seems to take more out of a dog than physical activity, limit at-home training sessions to about 10 minutes two or three times a day. And if you decide to enroll in a group class, look for instructors who break up each training session with play time or question-and-answer periods. (Many group classes last an hour or more.)

THE MOST CHALLENGING ASPECT OF BASIC

OBEDIENCE IS HELPING YOUR DOG

UNDERSTAND WHAT YOU WANT IT TO DO.

Positive Reinforcement

The instructional tools of basic obedience (lavish praise, food treats, collars of various types, leashes, and so on) are means to an end—verbal control over your dog. Almost all techniques incorporate operant conditioning, where the dog's correct response to a command (the stimulus) results in a reward (the reinforcement). This reward increases the probability that the dog will behave the same way next time. Without constant reinforcement, dogs gradually "forget" learned behaviors.

Deliver positive reinforcement immediately after each obeyed command. Verbal praise is always an appropriate form of positive reinforcement; a smile, a quick game of fetch, or food treats are also effective. The more valuable the reward (from the dog's point of view), the faster the initial learning.

For many dogs, food treats are the most valuable reward and the most compelling reinforcer. But once your dog learns a command, "randomize" treats, gradually replacing them with other reinforcements. If Pepper gets a food treat every time she sits on command, the reinforcement value of food diminishes. But if Pepper intermittently receives a treat, she'll be more likely to obey. Her motivation comes from not knowing when she'll get praise and a treat, or praise alone.

Key Commands

"The most important commands are those that will keep your dog out of trouble," says Dr. Nicholas Dodman. The big three are:

■ *"Come"—especially useful if your dog is running toward a busy road;*
■ *"Down"—which inactivates your dog in any situation;*
■ *"Leave it"—which discourages potentially harmful canine curiosity.*

Canine Correction

The good news is that you can raise a well-mannered family dog and still demonstrate considerable affection toward it—even to the point of "spoiling" it. The key is to treat your dog like the family member it is, while at the same time recognizing and respecting its "dog-ness." Harsh punishment is never necessary and is usually counterproductive—getting physical with a dominant-aggressive or an anxious dog will only aggravate the problem. Experts often distinguish between negative reinforcement—an aversive stimulus applied to increase the frequency of a desired behavior—and punishment applied after an undesirable action to decrease its frequency. To avoid confusion, we'll use the term "correction."

Because dogs are not born knowing how humans want them to behave, they usually exhibit some natural behavior, such as chewing or chasing, that we find unacceptable in certain circumstances. Consequently, many obedience training programs allow dogs to make mistakes so the trainer/owner can help the dog learn which behaviors are desirable—resulting in a reward—and which are undesirable—resulting in a correction.

Some trainers and animal behaviorists believe that dogs can learn basic obedience without correction. That's probably true for highly responsive dogs. Generally, your dog's personality, largely shaped by heredity and its early experience, will determine how much correction, if any, it needs during obedience training. For most dogs, a combination of positive reinforcement and appropriate correction will probably work best.

Effective correction asserts the handler's leadership; it should not inflict pain. Give corrections just as the animal begins the unwanted behavior. Corrections are most effective when the dog connects its own behavior—not the action of its handler—to the correction.

Correction can range from a frown or verbal reprimand, to a properly applied leash-and-collar correction, to "time out"—the owner's physical and emotional withdrawal. Withdrawing attention often gets better results than negative attention—as owners who yell to no avail at their barking dogs soon learn.

Two cardinal rules of correction: Never work with your dog when you're angry, and never discipline your dog unless you've clearly expressed what you want from it. Anger often leads to unnecessarily harsh correction. And inappropriate punishment is not only inhumane but a deterrent to training. Confused, anxious, fearful dogs are too distracted to learn.

Choosing a Trainer

Obedience training books and videos work well for young pups in the controlled atmosphere of your home, but most people and dogs eventually benefit from "live" instruction.

Some owners, especially those whose dogs have developed problematic behavior, opt for private, at-home training. Group classes, on the other hand, offer training for you and socialization for your dog. But the class size must be manageable. Although learning amid distractions is good preparation for real-life situations, you and your dog may get flustered in classes with more than 10 dogs per instructor.

Selecting the right instructor is a most important first step. Ask for referrals from dog-owning friends, your veterinarian, the local humane society, or the Better Business Bureau. Observe classes without your dog and look for smiling handlers and tail-wagging dogs.

Steer clear of trainers who blindly adhere to a single method. "Look for someone with the ability to apply a wide range of techniques," advises Brian Kilcommons, a noted dog trainer and author of Good Owners, Great Dogs. *"Be suspicious of trainers who say, 'This is the only way,' and of those who offer 'lifetime guarantees.'"*

The best trainers assess the particular needs of each dog-and-owner pair. Notice how much individual attention the trainer gives—especially to dogs and owners who are struggling.

Although several dog-training associations "certify" train-ers, there are currently no universal certification stan-dards. But you'll find the right trainer if you apply the criteria described above and remember that a trainer's communication skills and sense of humor are more important than paper credentials.

Lifetime of Learning

Sometimes dogs and their owners receive mortar boards and diplo-mas after completing a basic obedience class. Such ceremonies, while cute, are misleading. There is no "graduation" from obedience train-ing; it's a continual process. Your dog will more consistently obey if you use every interaction as an opportunity to reinforce training.

When Zeke comes to you seeking attention, make him sit or lie down before petting or playing. This "no free lunch" policy gently reminds your dog that you're in charge—while still giving the dog the positive attention it craves.

While basic obedience training requires time, energy, and pa-tience, it's much easier than trying to solve behavior problems later. Wouldn't you rather romp with your well-mannered pal than grap-ple with neighbors over your canine's unruly behavior? What's more, training is a great opportunity for you and your dog to reinforce your partnership. ❧

15

How Dogs Learn

Successful learning comes from the effective use of rewards and deterrents. Most canine "education" occurs through conditioning.

Dogs are constantly learning—even when no one is intentionally "teaching" them. When humans do endeavor to teach dogs—whether it's basic-obedience commands, complex agility-course maneuvers, or appropriate "manners"—successful learning comes from the effective use of rewards and deterrents.

Making Associations

Most canine "education" occurs through conditioning. Earlier this century, Russian psychologist Ivan Pavlov "discovered" classical conditioning. Pavlov observed that dogs naturally salivate when presented with food. After repeatedly pairing the presentation of food with a ringing bell, Pavlov conditioned dogs to salivate at the "ding" alone (a so-called conditioned response).

Dog owners frequently deal with the consequences of classical conditioning, though they may not realize it. Dogs that tremble with fear at the animal hospital have been classically conditioned to associate the sights, smells, and sounds of the clinic with unpleasant sensations—like the "pinch" that accompanies vaccination. Many veterinarians help their patients avoid this conditioned response by making visits as pleasant as possible—often using treats and petting to take the dog's mind off potentially uncomfortable procedures.

Housetraining is another example of classical conditioning. The innate response to a full bladder or bowel is to eliminate. Housetraining helps dogs associate these natural urges with the great outdoors. (You anticipate a pup's need to "go" and take it outside.)

When people praise dogs for eliminating outdoors, they're using operant conditioning—adding a reward to strengthen the association. Operant conditioning—the basis of obedience training—also underlies less desirable canine behavior such as begging for food. It is also the key to "training out" inappropriate behavior through behavior modification. In operant conditioning, dogs learn to respond to specific stimuli (such as an obedience command) in specific ways by associating their response with immediate reinforcement.

Do That Again!

A reinforcer is anything that increases the likelihood that a behavior will be repeated. There are basically two types—positive and negative. "A positive reinforcer is a pleasant consequence that encourages a dog to repeat a behavior," explains Dr. Nicholas Dodman, director of the Behavior Clinic at Tufts University School of Veterinary Medicine. You can use just about anything your dog likes or wants to do as a positive reinforcer

Positive reinforcers often used during obedience training include food treats, praise, toys, and petting. But sometimes, owners unintentionally positively reinforce "problem" behaviors.

For example, if you rebuke an attention-seeking dog for whining, you give the dog the attention it wants and encourage rather than discourage the behavior. And owners frequently positively reinforce fear in their dogs by coddling them in fear-provoking situations. Dogs quickly learn that fear pays off.

Puppies—adorable mental "sponges" that they are—are especially susceptible to developing problem behaviors through an owner's unintentional positive reinforcement. "When a puppy jumps on you, you're inclined to pick it up," notes Dennis Fetko, Ph.D., a California-based

applied animal behaviorist. "But doing so rewards the dog and encourages jumping behavior, which becomes a nuisance when the puppy grows into a 70-pound dog."

One way to extinguish bothersome behaviors a dog has learned through positive reinforcement is to completely halt further reinforcement. When the payoff for a behavior disappears, so does the behavior—eventually. But suddenly withdrawing reinforcement can temporarily intensify undesirable behavior. Owners therefore often find it difficult to follow through with this technique.

Despite its name, negative reinforcement also increases the frequency of a behavior. "A negative reinforcer is an unpleasant situation or sensation that an animal learns to avoid by behaving in a certain way," explains Dr. Dodman. For example, drivers learn to "buckle up" to silence the seat-belt buzzers in automobiles.

But negative reinforcement can also work against you. If you grant "early release" to a dog that's wriggling during a veterinary exam, this escape from restraint (the negative reinforcer) encourages the dog to struggle more the next time.

Learning the Don'ts

Punishment is an unpleasant consequence delivered after an undesirable behavior that decreases the likelihood the behavior will recur. Punishment should never entail pain. Often, all you need is a simple "time out"—isolating your dog from social contact right after misbehavior.

Punishment can backfire, though. If you don't apply it consistently to each and every misdemeanor, your occasional lapses become powerful reinforcers of the behavior. Also, some dogs become immune to punishment through habituation (the gradual extinction of a response after repeated exposure to a stimulus).

Timing Is Everything

Positive reinforcement and punishment have one thing in common: they must occur immediately after the behavior to work. (Dogs connect both reward and punishment with the last thing they did.) In fact, poorly timed punishment can actually discourage a desired behavior.

The classic example: a dog comes when called away from an indiscretion only to be punished for the indiscretion rather than rewarded for coming. The dog interprets this as punishment for coming and is less likely to obey future "come" commands.

The frequency of positive reinforcement is also important. "Continuous reinforcement is necessary to help a dog learn a new behavior," says Dr. Dodman. "But after the dog has learned the behavior, intermittent reinforcement more effectively maintains it because the dog never knows when the reward is coming."

Reinforcement Checklist

Positive reinforcement is the most powerful of canine learning tools. Here are some tips for getting the most from it:

■ Create an environment conducive to successful learning. For example, teach "come" in a fenced-in area, with your dog tethered to a long lead.

■ Attract your dog's attention by offering a variety of reinforcers from among its favorite foods, toys, and activities.

■ Don't give your dog free access to anything you use as a reinforcer. Doing so will diminish the potency of the reinforcer.

■ If you use edibles as reinforcers, give the dog small, quickly consumable tidbits to avoid satiation and a distracting focus on eating.

■ To make reinforcement virtually instantaneous, consider using a secondary reinforcer (such as a manual clicker). If you repeatedly make a clicking sound when delivering a primary reinforcer (such as food), eventually the click alone will positively reinforce the behavior.

Better Behavior

In addition to encouraging new and desirable behavior, positive reinforcement can also help your dog overcome some undesirable behaviors. If Cleo freaks out during thunderstorms, for example, you can expose her to the sound of thunder at a tolerably low volume. If you reward her calm tolerance of the sound with a tasty tidbit, you are conditioning her to associate the noise with a pleasant experience rather than fear, which we call counterconditioning.

If you continue reinforcing calm behavior while very gradually increasing the volume of the feared noise, Cleo eventually will become desensitized to thunder. But remember, even after Cleo has become desensitized, intermittent reinforcement will maintain the new learned behavior.

Rewarding Refusal

By itself, punishment teaches a dog only what not to do. The real goal, however, is to teach the dog what it should do. "The only reason to punish is so you don't have to punish again," says Dr. Fetko, who, like many behaviorists, recommends pairing punishment, if necessary, with the power of positive reinforcement.

For example, if an adult dog jumps on you, hold (don't squeeze) its paws. When the dog struggles to free itself, maintain your hold, walk the dog backward a few steps (an unnatural maneuver for canines), and push it away while saying "off." Then tease the dog to jump on you again. Repeat the hold, step-back, and push procedure until the dog refuses to jump. Then squat down and praise it for not jumping. "The power is in the reward," says Dr. Fetko, "so always praise such refusal lavishly."

Remember, when it comes to helping dogs learn, you should be more of a benevolent stage manager than a punishing tyrant. Figure out precisely what you want your dog to learn and then set up your pooch's environment so the proper learning events take place at the right times. And closely monitor your own actions—you don't want to reinforce behaviors you may later wish you hadn't. ❧

16

Imitation: Gateway to Learning

Imitation is only the first step in the learning process. Repeated practice and large doses of positive reinforcement must follow.

To us, imitation may be the "sincerest form of flattery," but to our canine chums, imitation is an early but important step in the multistage learning process. As many dog owners realize, however, imitation can lead to either beneficial or baneful outcomes. Anecdotal reports suggest that young sheepdogs with no prior interest in herding sheep may begin to imitate and learn their intended job after watching veteran herding dogs work. But this imitative influence can also work the other way. An adult dog watching a puppy chew on a couch might focus its attention on the couch and eventually join in.

Imitation and Survival

In the wild, learning through imitation makes perfect survival sense. "Theoretically, a young wolf that watches its parents hunt will learn more quickly how to capture prey than one that tries to figure it out on its own," notes Dr. Jean DeNapoli, a resident at the Behavior Clinic at Tufts University School of Veterinary Medicine.

Even among domesticated dogs, you can see imitative behavior at work. As soon as pups can walk, one member of the litter usually waddles out to explore, with the others following close behind. And once one pup in a litter has developed a skill through trial and error, the others often quickly learn it by mimicking the pioneering pup.

A puppy's mind soaks up information like a sponge during its first 12 to 16 weeks. Dogs deprived of the opportunity to interact with and imitate their littermates' play-and-scuffle behavior during this period of accelerated learning may have trouble relating to their own kind—and to people—later in life. "Puppies removed from the litter too early tend to exhibit inappropriate social behaviors," observes Stanley Coren, Ph.D., a professor of psychology at the University of British Columbia in Canada and author of *The Intelligence of Dogs.*

Even though the pace of learning slows as dogs age, older dogs still seem to use imitation as a springboard to learning. Remember, though, that dogs of any age can imitate both "good" and "bad" behaviors. A dog can learn undesirable habits—such as begging for food, stool eating (coprophagia), or furniture chewing—from an unruly canine comrade. For this reason, it's prudent to think twice before getting a canine companion to help "reform" a dog that is destructive when left alone. What you may view as a solution could actually compound the problem, resulting in two dogs that destroy the house while you're away.

Where's the Proof?

To date, the only scientific studies on imitative learning in companion animals involve the dog's feline counterpart. Cats that watch another cat press a bar to obtain a food reward learn to press the bar significantly faster than cats that haven't had a chance to observe such behavior. To try to prove that imitation-based learning occurs in dogs as well, investigators would have to set up a similar problem-solving situation with dogs and measure whether "observer" dogs consistently solved the problem faster than nonobservers.

Studies aside, dog lovers everywhere revel in telling anecdotes about dogs imitating other dogs—and people. Many of these stories center on working dogs like the aforementioned sheepdogs, but anecdotes about imitative behavior extend to household companions as well. For example, Barney and Charlie, two intrepid dog consultants, balked at using the doggie door their owner had installed, despite coaxing with their favorite treats. Not until their owner crawled through the door herself did Barney and Charlie figure out how to push through the doggie door.

Sometimes canine imitative behavior can be downright entertaining. Some of us have known operatic dogs that "sing along" with their owners—and not necessarily on key. Some owners also report that their dogs learned undoglike vocalizations—such as yodels—

after hearing another dog do the same thing.

And sometimes imitative behavior can save lives. According to Professor Coren, legend has it that the St. Bernards that rescue lost Alpine travelers learn their life-saving skills from one another. As the story goes, two dogs stay with the victim, and one goes in search of human help. Inexperienced Saints learn their roles as "stayers" or "goers" by trekking out with experienced dogs, not from human trainers.

Imitation and Instinct

Understanding the role of imitation in canine learning is complicated by the fact that dogs can't tell us what part of their learning process has the most impact on them. And it's often difficult to distinguish among the different pathways to learning, such as imitation, instinct, and social facilitation (the influence of group behavior on social animals). According to Dr. Katherine Houpt, director of the Behavior Clinic at Cornell University's College of Veterinary Medicine, dogs that bark more, bark longer, or bark with less provocation when in the presence of another barking dog (or dogs) are probably vocalizing more out of social camaraderie than from imitative impulses. Along similar lines, while many breeders note that male dogs are more likely to breed if they've observed another male animal breed, "this may be more a matter of instinctive arousal than imitation," says Dr. Houpt.

Another area of learning where instinct and imitation tend to blur is housetraining. Some owners and trainers believe that one of the easiest ways to housetrain a young dog is to have an already housetrained dog escort the newcomer outside. On the other hand, many people recount incidents of previously housetrained adult dogs suddenly "regressing" when an unhousetrained puppy enters the home. "That kind of inappropriate elimination is probably less imitation and more a response to the scent of the other dog," says Dr. Houpt.

And "regressive" housesoiling is more likely to occur if you introduce a puppy into a home with an older dog that has never been 100-percent housetrained or shows visible distress at the new pup's arrival. One way to prevent regression in an older dog—and to successfully housetrain any dog—is to get the animal outdoors before accidents happen indoors. Always remember to praise the dog enthusiastically for doing its "business" outside.

Leveraging Imitative Behavior

There are easier ways to teach your dog to sit than by squatting on your haunches and encouraging Fido to imitate you. But in certain situations, you can help your dog learn new behaviors by taking advantage of its inclination to imitate. For example, you can use imitation to help "civilize" an obstreperous canine newcomer if you have an already obedient dog in residence. When you say, "Doggies, come!," the well-trained animal will, of course, come—and the newcomer will most likely follow.

Many people who train dogs for agility competitions deliberately jump over hurdles and crawl through tunnels to focus their canine teammates' attention on the obstacles at hand. Stanley Coren, Ph.D., a professor of psychology at the University of British Columbia in Canada and author of The Intelligence of Dogs, *has observed that dogs just starting out in group obedience training learn faster when they watch advanced classes at work. "Novices that don't have a chance to watch the more experienced dogs in training don't seem to learn as quickly," he observes.*

You may also be able to curb certain canine behavior problems by imitating your dog's body language to get your point across. According to Patricia McConnell, Ph.D., a certified applied animal behaviorist, the most frequent human response to a dog that jumps up is to manually push it away. "Usually, dogs respond to a hand push by jumping up again because they think you're playing with them," observes Dr. McConnell.

She recommends a firm blocking movement using your upper torso and shoulder. "This imitation of a canine 'body block' is an effective and nonaggressive way of saying, 'This space is mine, not yours,'" concludes Dr. McConnell.

Just the Beginning

Imitation may set the stage for both job-related learning and nifty dog tricks, but don't expect to teach your dog by relying on imitation alone. Dogs are most likely to learn behaviors when they get plenty of positive reinforcement and practice as part of the learning process. Nonetheless, keep a watchful eye on imitative canine behavior in your household because, even without your approval, dogs are just as likely to imitate behaviors you don't want as those you do. ❧

17

A Little Goes a Long Way

Consistency is absolutely necessary when obedience-training a dog. The commands you use must also be simple and consistent.

The vast majority of domestic dogs are well-mannered family members at home and good canine citizens in the community. Their behavior is the product of a complex interplay between genetics and environmental influences (including health care, nutrition, and relationships with other dogs and people). There is little doubt that human actions and reactions can influence a dog's behavior—both positively and negatively. When our dogs behave well, we can take some of the credit; but when they don't — when they "act out"—we have to look at how we influence their mischief-making. Don't feel too guilty—minor alterations in your behavior can have a positive impact on your dog's behavior.

Human Behavioral Cues

Even the most subtle human behavioral cues can reinforce good manners or exacerbate behavior problems such as dominance aggression and separation anxiety. "But because both genetic and other forces are at work, people aren't entirely responsible for either good or bad behavior in their dogs," emphasizes Dr. Nicholas Dodman, professor and director of the Behavior Clinic at Tufts University School of Veterinary Medicine.

The totality of a dog's genetics and environment produces canine behavior—for better or for worse. For example, a dog born to temperamentally sound parents, socialized fully with other dogs, and nurtured carefully by its human stewards has the potential for "greatness" as a family companion. But a different mix of "ingredients" is likely to produce a different behavioral outcome.

Consistency Is Key

We all know that many dogs and owners communicate with one another as if they were members of the same species. (How many times have you waxed philosophical with your dog, and how many times has your dog "talked" you into a game of fetch with a playful yip and its familiar play bow?) Such "sixth sense" communication often leads to intense emotional attachments between dogs and their people. (Not surprisingly, psychologists have noted elements of "significant other" or parent-child relationships in intense dog-owner relationships.) But along with these powerful attachments often come some of the same "ups and downs" you see in a human family. And these ups and downs can sometimes perplex our pooches.

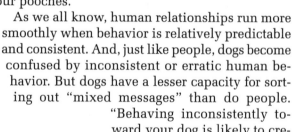

As we all know, human relationships run more smoothly when behavior is relatively predictable and consistent. And, just like people, dogs become confused by inconsistent or erratic human behavior. But dogs have a lesser capacity for sorting out "mixed messages" than do people. "Behaving inconsistently toward your dog is likely to create a state of conflict in the dog," explains Valerie O'Farrell, Ph.D., a psychologist and animal behaviorist affiliated with the University of Edinburgh's School for Veterinary Studies in Scotland. Dr. O'-Farrell says owners who are very loving toward their dog one moment and irritable the next confuse the dog and may set off anxiety behaviors such as compulsive disorders or separation anxiety. (If you're angry or upset about something, try to unwind a bit before interacting with your dog.)

Consistency (not to mention simplicity) is absolutely necessary when obedience training a dog If you sometimes reprimand your dog rather than praise it for coming when called, the dog may think twice about dashing in your direction next time you call it. But such apparent recalcitrance is a normal canine response to inconsistent treatment.

The training commands you use must also be simple and consistent. The command "Sit!" will get your dog's fanny on the ground faster than the metaphysical query "Why won't you sit for me?"

A RECENT UNPUBLISHED STUDY SUGGESTS

THAT PEOPLE WHO ARE DRIVEN BY

FEELINGS (THOSE WHO "LIVE IN THEIR

HEARTS") ARE MORE LIKELY TO FOSTER

DOMINANT-AGGRESSIVE BEHAVIOR IN DOGS

THAN THOSE WHO ARE FACT- OR LOGIC-

DRIVEN (THOSE WHO "LIVE IN THEIR HEADS")

Discouraging Dominance

Aggression is the number-one reported canine behavior problem. And aggression often stems from a dog's attempt to dominate other members of its family But how does human behavior influence a dog's aggressive quest for "top dog" status?

While some dogs inherit a predisposition toward dominance, Dr. Dodman has observed that "kindly, compliant owners who don't set limits and who identify with their dog more as a person than a dog can encourage dominance." Similarly, in a study involving 50 owners, Dr. O'Farrell noticed increased dominant-aggressive behavior in dogs whose owners were involved "anthropomorphically" with them. (Anthropomorphism is the tendency to attribute human characteristics or motivations to animals.) "A dog predisposed to dominance is more likely to exert that dominance over its owner if the owner gives in to its every demand," explains Dr. O'Farrell.

Early analysis of a recent unpublished study suggests that people who are driven by feelings (those who "live in their hearts") are more likely to foster dominant-aggressive behavior in dogs than those who are fact- or logic-driven (those who "live in their heads"). While it's difficult (perhaps impossible) for people to change their personality type, just a few simple changes in your interactions with a dominance-prone dog can often keep aggressive behavior in check.

Many behaviorists encourage owners to adopt a consistent "no free lunch" policy to modify dominant-aggressive behavior. A dominant dog should get what it wants the old-fashioned way: by earning it. Remember, you have at your fingertips most of the resources your dog wants and needs—food, water, access to the great outdoors, and attention. "With a dominant dog, it's best to supply these things only when the dog promptly and obediently responds to a command," says Dr. Dodman. When a dog is obedient, it is acknowledging that you are in charge.

But this strategic rationing of "goodies" makes some owners uneasy because they feel they are being "unkind." Gently insisting that your dog perform certain tasks (such as sitting and staying before eating or going for a walk) is not heartless. You have to set such expectations with dominance-prone dogs to establish who the leader is. The average "bossy" dog respects (in fact, prefers) clear-cut directives.

Spare the Rod

Still, some people find it hard to make changes in their behavior in order to improve their dog's manners. Hence, owners need ongoing support while navigating their way through behavior-modification programs. "It's important for the behaviorist to encourage the owner when he or she has made improvements and to gently draw attention to areas that need more work," says Dr. Dodman.

Remember—relatively minor changes in your behavior can create significant changes in your dog. (You don't have to undergo a personality makeover!) If you find your dog misbehaving, try to change some of the small interactions to point your dog in a more "mannerly" direction. ❖

Section IV

Behavior Problems
and Solutions

18

The Shy Dog

Acting submissively can help dogs maintain peaceful social order. But sometimes shyness becomes extreme and causes behavior problems.

Just like people, some dogs are more outgoing than others. When people describe a dog as "shy," "they usually refer to an animal that's submissive," says Dr. Gerry Flannigan, a resident at the Behavior Clinic at Tufts University School of Veterinary Medicine. Acting submissively in appropriate circumstances—such as when greeting a dominant dog or interacting with human "pack" members—helps canines maintain peaceful social order. But sometimes shyness becomes so extreme that behavior problems ensue.

Body-language Tipoffs

Like their reserved human counterparts, shy dogs have a certain "look." They usually avoid staring at or interacting with unfamiliar people or dogs. Shy dogs also often assume the "canine crouch"— hunching their shoulders and dropping their heads, ears, and tails—in an attempt to make themselves less conspicuous.

Sometimes, a shy dog's tucked tail will also wag. "Tail wagging suggests a heightened state of arousal, which may just as likely arise from ambivalence or extreme concentration as from cheerfulness," notes Dr. Nicholas Dodman. Consequently, if any tail-wagging dog also growls, raises its hackles, and bares its teeth, heed the signals coming from the pooch's head end.

Rather than exhibiting aggression, some very shy dogs (usually young females) urinate while assuming submissive postures. Submissive urination is the ultimate canine expression of deference in the presence of a dominant dog or person.

Nature and Nurture: Fifty-fifty

Some dogs are naturally aloof but quite self-confident. For example, many herding dogs (such as Shetland sheepdogs and border collies) and working dogs (such as boxers and mastiffs) are often reserved toward—but not afraid of—strangers.

Laid upon its inherited temperament "template," a dog's experiences—especially those early in life—also help determine how forward or retiring it is. A dog that has many pleasant encounters with people during the behaviorally pliant "sensitive period" (from about the third to sixteenth week of life) is far more likely to confidently engage with humans than a pup that has been inappropriately sheltered or exposed to adverse experiences.

Unpleasant early experiences can make some dogs wary around people in general. Others shy away from particular folks—most often men and children. In *The Dog Who Loved Too Much*, Dr. Dodman tells of a pup that retained a permanent fear of white-bearded men after being mistreated only once by a man with a white beard. But it could've been worse. For some dogs, a similar fearful episode mushrooms into fear of all "furry faced" men—or of all masculine personages.

Select Carefully

Because there's a significant experiential component to timidity, it's difficult to predict whether a young pup will turn into a shy adult. "You can usually identify pups in a litter that are super submissive or very aggressive," notes Dr. Flannigan, "but beyond that, behaviors displayed at 7 or 8 weeks can change significantly over time."

Still, if you don't want a shy dog, don't select a pup that refuses to follow you or romp with its littermates—despite how sorry you may feel for its "underdog" status. Also, because parents genetically pass on behavioral tendencies, you can get some idea of a pup's future temperament from examining its parents' "outlook on life."

PUNISHING A SHY DOG MAKES IT MORE—

NOT LESS—INSECURE.

Confidence Builders

To help develop a pup's self-confidence and social skills, enroll your youngster in puppy kindergarten, assuring first that all the canine participants are up to date on their vaccinations. Such gatherings expose pups to many other dogs and people and provide ideal opportunities to reward puppy poise and to nip socialization problems in the bud.

Many people adopt an adult dog that's already mildly to moderately shy. If you want to help such a pooch come out of its shell, let it pass through doorways ahead of you and win at competitive games like tug of war. (Behaviorists recommend against playing confrontational games with dogs on the dominant end of the canine behavior continuum.) "Always initiate and terminate these games yourself, and stop immediately if there's any sign of aggression," cautions Dr. Flannigan.

Another way to build canine confidence is to use the "jolly routine"—a term coined by animal behaviorist William Campbell, author of *Behavior Problems in Dogs*. At the first sign of insecurity in your dog, let the pooch know there's nothing to worry about by happily clapping your hands or bouncing a ball while laughing or emitting other upbeat utterances.

Desensitization/Counterconditioning

For dogs with higher levels of fear and shyness, you'll probably need to employ the behavior-modification duo of desensitization and counterconditioning. During desensitization, you expose your dog to the feared entity (or a creative facsimile thereof) at very low, gradually increasing levels of intensity. If your dog's afraid of men in uniform, for example, introduce, at some distance, someone in a uniform who induces very little fear (a woman, perhaps). Gradually move your assistant closer to the dog (or vice versa) until the dog remains unfazed with her at arm's-length proximity. Next, introduce a casually dressed man at a distance, and again gradually reduce the space separating person and dog. Finally, repeat the process with a uniformed man. Throughout each step, close the distance gap very gradually so the dog never experiences full-blown distress.

Counterconditioning boosts desensitization by helping your dog "feel good" amid fearful stimuli. During exposure to the feared entity, give your dog a simple command (such as "sit" or "watch me") and offer it highly attractive rewards when it obeys. The anticipation of receiving a favorite toy or treat helps the dog overcome its discomfort.

Unfortunately, effectively desensitizing and counterconditioning a fearful dog can take months of painstaking work. Plus, desensitized dogs may relapse unless they're periodically exposed to fear-inducing stimuli, so you may need to give your dog abbreviated refresher courses from time to time.

Whichever confidence-building technique you use, it's counterproductive to either coddle or punish a shy dog. Dogs perceive coddling as a reward for whatever behavior they're engaging in, and punishing a shy dog makes it more—not less—insecure.

Should you want or need to, you can gently and lovingly raise your dog's position on the sociability scale within the boundaries of its genetically programmed temperament. But unless your dog's shyness leads to submissive urination, aggression, or some other genuine behavior problem, just love your pooch for who he or she is.

When Timidity Turns to Aggression

Unlike dominant-aggressive dogs that lash out at family members, fear-aggressive dogs usually direct their antisocial behavior at strangers—such as delivery people or children who innocently wander into their space. Because this type of aggressive behavior is rooted in fear, these assaults often come from behind.

Fear aggression is really a type of fight-or-flight behavior that can be triggered when a fearful dog feels trapped—such as when it's tethered, cornered, or otherwise prevented from running away. Like other forms of aggression, fear aggression is mediated by physiological changes set off by the dog's autonomic (involuntary) nervous system. These include dilated pupils, raised hackles, and increases in heart rate, blood pressure, and blood-sugar levels.

The body language of fear-aggressive dogs often sends out mixed messages. Such dogs may crouch submissively and tuck their tails, but their hackles are usually raised, and they often growl and bare their teeth menacingly.

"The motto of these so-called 'shy-sharp' pooches is 'a good offense is the best defense,'" says Dr. Nicholas Dodman. These dogs gradually learn that a well-timed growl or snap causes people to back off—exactly what the pooches want—making fear aggression a self-reinforcing behavior. Unfortunately, self-reinforcing behaviors are often the most difficult to modify.

Of course, the best way to counter fear-related aggression is to prevent it from developing in the first place. That means careful dog selection and plenty of socialization with people. Through no fault of their own, many fear-aggressive dogs have a "checkered past," including abuse, neglect, and/or lack of socialization.

While the desensitization and counterconditioning techniques can quell the fear that leads to aggression, owners who try to retrain fear-aggressive dogs risk injury to themselves and others. For this reason, such dogs should be kept on a leash when other people are around, and owners should enlist the help of a qualified professional. In addition to helping you implement behavior-modification techniques, a veterinarian may also prescribe nonsedating medications (such as buspirone or fluoxetine) to help accelerate the learning process. In the past, before the introduction of these mood-stabilizing drugs, veterinarians sometimes tranquilized fear-aggressive dogs. But it's much more effective to teach a dog not to be afraid than to mask a dog's fear and aggression with tranquilizers. 🐾

19

Fears & Phobias

*Knowing when your dog is afraid and helping
it overcome dysfunctional fears will help
both of you live more peacefully.*

L
ike many behaviors, fear—that "hardwired" whole-body
response to anything scary or dangerous—can be a life-
saving adaptation. It has saved many an animal from death
or injury by spurring them to react to danger by fighting,
fleeing, or freezing motionless.

But among our canine companions, fearful responses—ranging
from mild anxiety to full-blown phobia (a response disproportion-
ate to the actual danger)—often exceed what's necessary for survival.

Triangle of Fear

Just what are dogs afraid of? According to Dr. Nicholas Dodman, the
canine "triangle of fear" consists of:

■ Fear of the animate, including people and other animals—sometimes even insects.
■ Fear of the inanimate, including noises such as thunder, textures
such as slippery linoleum floors, and sights such as tarpaulins blow-
ing in the wind.
■ Fear of situations, including car rides, visits to the veterinarian,
and separation from owners.

Dogs that are afraid of a particular person, thing, or situation often
generalize their fear by associating elements of an original trauma

with similar people, things, or situations. For example, many thunder-phobic dogs are also terrified of fireworks or backfiring automobiles. A dog mistreated by a bearded man may become terrified of all bearded men—or even of all men. Puppies attacked by aggressive older dogs often retain a lifelong fear of their canine brethren. And a dog that has had its hair yanked by an unsupervised toddler may skitter under the bed at the sight or sound of young children.

To complicate matters further, fear often involves more than one point on the triangle. Many dogs afraid of thunder, for example, also show signs of separation anxiety. Moreover, categorizing phobias is not always clear cut. One canine patient that appeared to have a situational fear (once outside, it was terrified to go back in the house) really had a sound phobia: the dog feared the squawking of the newest family member—a parrot.

The Face of Fear

An anxious dog may whine, pant, or pace with its ears back and its pupils dilated. As its level of fear increases, the dog may shake, tremble, and assume a submissive posture. Truly phobic dogs may attempt to escape from a perceived danger (sometimes with injurious consequences) or lose bladder or bowel control. In a small percentage of dogs afraid of people, fear manifests itself as aggression. Such "people phobic" dogs may bite when they sense that fleeing is impossible.

The fear your dog shows on the outside reflects a cascade of internal biochemical processes. The "fight or flight" (sympathetic) branch of the autonomic nervous system mediates the release of various hormones (including adrenaline) that prepare a dog's body for the quick release of energy. "The dog's heart pumps faster, blood is diverted away from the digestive tract and toward the skeletal muscles, blood sugar levels rise, and the bronchial tubes in the lungs dilate," explains Dr. Dodman.

Any healthy dog may display a fear response, but certain breeds and strains seem more innately susceptible to fear than others. Still, it's usually an actual experience—activating whatever genetically installed "fear equipment" your dog has—that triggers fearful behavior. Fears resulting from trauma or isolation during the first 12 to 14 weeks of a dog's life are particularly tenacious. But Dr. Dodman points out that "if something emotionally traumatic happens to a dog at any age, the event can leave an indelible impression and cause a lasting fear."

PREVENTING FEAR IS FAR EASIER THAN

TEACHING DOGS NOT TO BE AFRAID OF

THINGS THAT ALREADY FRIGHTEN THEM.

Treating Fears and Phobias

Preventing fear is far easier (and less tedious) than teaching dogs not to be afraid of things that already frighten them. Consequently, experts recommend gradually exposing young puppies to as many sights, sounds, and smells as possible—and making these experiences as pleasant as possible by offering praise, petting, and treats.

If your dog has acquired a fear or two along the way, the first step toward effective treatment is to identify specifically what generates fear in your dog. Although pinpointing the original trauma may provide some insight, that information is not always crucial to successful treatment. Usually, all you need to know is what your dog fears now and how it behaves when afraid.

Your sympathetic reactions to your dog's fear may actually make matters worse. Owners who fuss over their phobic dogs inadvertently teach their animals to associate coddling with fear behavior. Conversely, punishing a dog that has behaved inappropriately out of fear—for example, by destroying household furnishings while in the throes of separation anxiety—makes the dog even more nervous.

No matter what your dog is afraid of, the most universally and successfully applied treatment approach combines two behavior-modification techniques—desensitization and counterconditioning. (A few animal behaviorists claim success with a technique called "flooding"—unrelenting exposure to the feared stimulus at full intensity. But most experts deem flooding inhumane, and it also carries the risk of making the phobia worse.)

■ Desensitization

During desensitization, you expose your dog to the fearful stimulus (or a creative approximation of it) at very low, then gradually increasing, levels of intensity. The trick is to start with a mild stimulus and increase its intensity so gradually that the dog never experiences full-blown fear during the training process. For example, many owners of thunder-phobic dogs have successfully desensitized their dogs by exposing them to low-volume recordings of thunderstorms, gradually increasing the volume until the dogs tolerate naturally occurring thunderstorms without signs of fear. It's best to desensitize thunder-phobes during the winter months, when there's little or no chance of real thunderstorms. Also, you may have to add a strobe light to the desensitization program because many thunder-phobic dogs associate lightning with thunder—and fear both.

For a dog afraid of certain people, distance is the factor you must vary. Begin with someone who induces no (or very mild) fear. For example, if your dog is afraid of men, bring a woman into the dog's view—but far enough away so the woman causes no anxiety. Then, gradually move her closer to the dog (or vice versa). When the dog is comfortable with a woman at close proximity, introduce a man— but at a distance. "Any time the dog experiences a fear reaction, go back a few steps, and then continue to work forward slowly," cautions Dr. Dodman.

■ Counterconditioning

Counterconditioning boosts the effects of desensitization by helping the dog "feel good" while confronting a fearful stimulus. As you gradually introduce the agent of fear, simultaneously offer attractive rewards if the dog remains calm. Pairing the sound of distant thunder, for example, with delectable food treats creates positive associations between the noise and tasty tidbits. (For the rare dog not motivated by food, try a favorite toy, activity, or any reward more powerful than the fear.)

While the counterconditioning-desensitization approach usually works, it is not an instant solution (and fears that are more genetic than experiential in origin are less responsive). Because you must very gradually increase the stimulus intensity (and because a full-blown fear reaction—either during or outside of training sessions— can take you back to "square one"), an effective program can take months to complete. Also, fear-desensitized dogs sometimes relapse. After initial desensitization, if your dog has no exposure to the agent of fear for a period of time, you should take it through an abbreviated "refresher" course.

Medicinal Aids

In certain cases, medication can facilitate behavior-modification techniques. "Because medication can accelerate progress, pharmacological support often helps owners follow through with the behavioral part of the program," says Dr. Petra Mertens, a resident at the Behavior Clinic at Tufts University School of Veterinary Medicine.

Not long ago, benzodiazepines (such as Valium™) and phenothiazines (such as Thorazine™) were the predominant "pharmacological shoehorns" for phobic dogs. But these drugs are not without counterproductive side effects. Although the drugs often calm fears, they also sedate patients, thus stalling behavior modification.

Today, veterinarians have an array of effective, nonsedating medications at their disposal. One such drug is propranolol, a beta blocker. Beta blockers inhibit the sympathetic nervous system, making the dog physiologically calmer.

Also effective are the antianxiety drugs buspirone and fluoxetine—the latter commonly known as Prozac™. Through different chemical mechanisms, both drugs modify the action of the neurotransmitter serotonin in the brain. (Remember, dogs don't react uniformly to a particular psychoactive drug at a particular dosage, so it's a good idea to carefully monitor your dog's response the first few times you administer such drugs.)

If you have a phobic dog, take heart. Although it may not be as simple as convincing a frightened child that monsters don't lurk under the bed, there's a good chance that you can help your dog overcome its unreasonable fears. But you'll need patience, consistency, and possibly some professional guidance. And if you're just starting out with a young puppy, select one from parents known not to be unduly fearful. Then expose the pup to as many new situations and people as you can. ❧

20

Nervous About Noises

Some dogs react phobically to "everyday" noises— the whirr of household appliances, the rumble of heavy traffic, or things that go "bang."

Your dog's acute hearing can be both a blessing and a curse. While it enables Fido to hear the fridge door open despite a cacophony of other sounds, it may also cause your dog anxiety amid loud noises such as thunder or fireworks. A few dogs even have noise phobias—intense fear reactions to sound.

No one knows why noise phobias develop. But according to Dr. Nicholas Dodman, director of the Behavior Clinic at Tufts University School of Veterinary Medicine, these phobias most often show up in northern sled-type dogs and larger sporting dogs that are nervous as youngsters. "During middle age, some loud event occurs, setting off a precipitous plunge into noise phobia," Dr. Dodman explains. Thunder-phobia is the most common example, but fear of thunder can generalize into fear of similar sounds, such as backfiring cars and sonic booms.

Spectrum of Fear

Dogs with mild noise-related anxiety tuck their tails and skittishly scan the environment. They may also tremble and seek attention from a human "protector." Moderately affected dogs quake, whimper, pace, pant, and seek shelter—often under a bed or in the bathroom. A severely noise-phobic dog will make frantic attempts to escape the sound, sometimes hurling itself at doors or windows.

DESENSITIZATION AND
COUNTERCONDITIONING ARE THE "GOLD
STANDARD" TREATMENTS FOR CANINE
NOISE PHOBIAS.

Volume Down, Patience Up

Desensitization is one proven treatment for noise sensitivity. Expose your dog to the "sinister" sound (or a simulation thereof) at a low enough volume so the animal shows no sign of apprehension. As long as the dog remains calm, reinforce the behavior with treats or toys so the dog associates the once-dreaded noise with agreeable experiences (counterconditioning). If your dog tolerates the low-volume exposure, continue to expose it to louder and louder versions of the sound and also continue rewarding calm behavior. Proceed to higher volumes very gradually and only after the dog shows no anxiety at a lower intensity. Continue until the animal tolerates the sound full-blast without becoming ruffled.

Alas, desensitization is easier said than done. The painstaking process may require several months of 10- to 20-minute sessions three times a week. And during desensitization, you must shield your dog from noise-phobic reactions to either real or simulated sound—or risk having to start the entire process from scratch. That's why wintertime—when Nature's "big bangs" from thunderstorms are rare—is the best time to treat canine noise phobias.

Prior to the first desensitization session, make sure the simulated noise (a recording, for example), delivered at full volume, sparks your dog's fear reaction. To achieve sufficiently realistic sound reproduction, you may have to invest in or borrow sophisticated sound equipment and/or specialized recordings.

Also, fear tends to be location-specific, so if you sound-desensitize your dog in the living room, you may have to repeat the process in other areas of your home. And because thunderstorms involve sensory ingredients other than thunder—such as the sound of wind and the flash of lightning—you may need to simulate multiple environmental conditions to completely desensitize your dog. Thunderstorms involve a complex of stimuli, so you may have to desensitize your storm-phobic dog to flashes of light in addition to the sounds of thunder, wind, and rain.

Because desensitization is so time-consuming, some veterinarians prescribe antianxiety medication as adjunctive treatment. "Drugs such as buspirone may help a noise-phobic dog stay calm and speed the desensitization process," says Dr. Dodman.

Weather Phenomena

Because decreases in barometric pressure and increases in static electricity accompany thunderstorms, some behaviorists speculate that dogs unresponsive to desensitization may sense these hard-to-simulate weather conditions and associate them with the negative experience of thunderstorms.

Lead, Don't Coddle

Because of the hereditary component of noise phobias, there are no sure-fire preventives. However, it's best to address any noise sensitivity early, before a full-blown noise phobia develops. Avoid coddling a dog that's anxious about noises. "Leadership is much better than sympathy," says Dr. Dodman. "If your dog seems afraid of a specific noise, turn its attention toward play or do some obedience exercises."

You may also forestall the development of noise phobias by exposing puppies to many noises (while rewarding them with treats) during their first few critical months of development. They'll soon associate noise with pleasure rather than fear. ❧

21

Overcoming
Separation Anxiety

Behavior modification combined with a new medication specifically for dogs with separation anxiety can make home life happier for everyone.

If he whines pitifully as you prepare to leave, barks frantically as you go out the door, and tears the place apart while you're gone, your dog is suffering from separation anxiety. The condition affects as many as an estimated 14 percent of the 54 million dogs in the U.S. and has been a leading cause of dogs being placed for adoption or euthanized.

For a dog suffering from separation anxiety, being apart from his owner is, quite simply, unbearable. In his frantic attempts to escape barriers such as door frames, window sills, and furniture, he can do tremendous damage to his surroundings as well as serious injury to himself.

Veterinary behaviorists report that separation anxiety accounts for approximately 20- to 40 percent of the cases they encounter, second only to aggression. To treat the disorder, some behaviorists use a combination of behavior training and medication. Anti-depressants and anti-anxiety medication developed for humans—prescribed in much smaller doses—have helped dogs overcome separation anxiety. Once their anxiety level decreased, dogs with separation anxiety responded better to behavior training.

Recently the U.S. Food and Drug Administration approved Clomicalm™, the first behavioral medication developed specifically for dogs with separation anxiety. Clomicalm, the trade name for clomipramine hydrochloride, is an antidepressant used for obsessive-compulsive disorder in humans.

Clomicalm, along with Anipryl™, a medication developed by the animal health division of the pharmaceutical firm Pfizer for canine senility or cognitive dysfunction syndrome, are the first behavioral medications subjected to clinical field studies and approved specifically for dogs by the USDA.

BEHAVIOR MODIFICATION BY THE OWNER
OF AN ANXIOUS DOG CAN HAVE AN
ENORMOUS IMPACT ON THE DOG'S
BEHAVIOR.

Dogs Who Love Too Much

Dr. Nicholas Dodman, director of Tufts Behavior Clinic, eloquently describes separation anxiety in his book, *The Dog Who Loved Too Much: Tales, Treatments, and the Psychology of Dogs.*

Dogs who suffer from the condition, Dr. Dodman writes, "become so closely bonded to their owners that they virtually have to be pried off them, and parting is not, as the saying goes, such sweet sorrow, but more of a living hell."

Dogs with separation anxiety may follow their owners from room to room, and curl up on the couch with them to watch TV. They seem to be happy only in their owners' presence, lacking the sense of independence they need to cope with being alone. Instead, once the owner leaves, a dog with separation anxiety will become frustrated by barriers, chewing the woodwork, window sills, destroying blinds or curtains, pacing back and forth. Food is rarely a distraction; frequently, dogs who suffer from separation anxiety refuse even to eat in their owners' absence.

These dogs are often gentle, doting, and sweet-natured, Dr. Dodman says, but the anxiety-related havoc they wreak in their owners' absence is sometimes misconstrued as being malicious, vindictive or retributive.

It does no good to punish the dog once you return—and the damage is already done—punishment only confuses an already anxious and distraught dog. Owners of a dog suffering from separation anxiety need to understand that he's not being willfully destructive or malicious. His behavior is caused by a trauma the dog suffered as a puppy, either physical or through neglect. Often such dogs were separated from their mother at a far too early age.

Dr. Dodman notes that dogs acquired from a pound are prime candidates for separation anxiety, and owners often act as enablers. Dogs with separation anxiety are so affectionate—who can resist the overly effusive tail wagging of a dog who's ecstatic to see you—they are especially appealing. Unfortunately some owners don't understand the potential for long-term difficulties.

Signs of Separation Anxiety

For most owners, the presence of serious, chronic separation anxiety is obvious. They just need to hear the complaints from their neighbors or look at the damage their dog has done around house. However, there are signs that separation anxiety is present that may be less obvious. All signs occur only in the real or apparent absence of the owner. Listed from the most to the least obvious:

■ *Destruction* ■ *Defecation* ■ *Urination* ■ *Loud, disruptive barking and howling* ■ *Licking with skin and fur irritation* ■ *Salivation with saliva staining* ■ *Salivation without saliva staining* ■ *Soft, nondisruptive barking and crying* ■ *Occasional anorexia* ■ *Pacing* ■ *Withdrawal*

Additionally, dogs with separation anxiety generally follow their owners almost continually and have long-lasting reunion rituals.

If you observe these symptoms and find them worrisome, speak to your veterinarian.

Hard Living?

"Detailed histories of dogs with separation anxiety often reveal 'dysfunctional' puppyhoods," says Dr. Nicholas Dodman. Almost all of the dogs Dr. Dodman has treated for this disorder have one common denominator: emotional trauma in their past. This trauma often involves early separation from mother and littermates, lack of human contact during the impressionable first 16 weeks of life, or a series of attachments to and separations from people. In some cases, a single traumatic event, such as the hospitalization of an owner, can precipitate separation anxiety in a dog.

But the fact that many "hard living" pups develop into normal, well-adjusted dogs suggests that internal factors also contribute to separation anxiety. In a recent study at the University of Pennsylvania School of Veterinary Medicine, most of the 45 canine subjects that exhibited separation anxiety didn't overtly fit the dysfunctional profile, according to Dr. Karen Overall, director of the veterinary school's Behavior Clinic. And, while it's been suggested that intense owner-dog attachments may contribute to separation anxiety, experts note that many coddled, "spoiled rotten" dogs tolerate solitude calmly. This evidence has led most animal behaviorists to conclude that some dogs are born with a genetic abnormality that predisposes them to high anxiety.

Behavior Modifications

Since owners are often—intentionally or not—part of the problem, it's imperative that they be part of the solution. Behavior modification by the owner of an anxious dog can have an enormous impact on the dog's behavior. In fact, during clinical field trials of Clomicalm, 55% of the dogs treated with behavior modification alone improved after eight weeks, compared to 65 percent of the dogs that received medication and behavior training.

Daily walks and romping for at least 20 to 30 minutes are recommended for much needed aerobic exercise. Games like tug of war can help build a dog's confidence if he gets to win. Changing the dog's food to a low protein brand will also help curb his excess energy.

If you're the owner of a dog with separation anxiety, decreasing your dog's dependence on you may be the biggest challenge you'll face. Recognizing that the dog's anxiety is destructive to a long and healthy relationship should be a strong incentive in proceeding with a program of behavior modification. It may be comforting to know that you don't have to act like an ogre towards your dog in treating the condition. Though you need to be firm and supportive, you should, at least **temporarily, adopt an attitude of nonchalance** towards your dog.

Ask any parent who's given in to a toddler's sobs at being left with a trusted babysitter or childcare provider; the more matter of fact you are the easier it eventually becomes for the transition to occur. Instead of showing your own worries about what will happen in your absence, act as though it's not a big deal as you prepare to leave the house. As part of Dr. Dodman's treatment for separation anxiety, he prescribes **ignoring a dog for at least 20 minutes before leaving and after returning.**

Since there are usually lots of cues to your departure—putting on your shoes, picking up your keys or your coat—it's helpful to desensitize your dog by running through these acts several times without actually leaving. In the evening, for example, pick up your keys and head for the door. Your dog will become a bit agitated, but will see that you're not really leaving, and settle down. Doing this a few times every night will eventually take the stress out of your actual departure.

When you come home, just as before you leave, ignore your dog for 15 to 20 minutes. "This evens out the emotional roller coaster ride these dogs experience with overly emotional departures and exuberant greetings from owners when they come home," says Dr. Dodman. "When your departures and returns generate less anxiety and excitement, your dog will begin to feel less tension in your absence."

While You're Away

Giving the dog a pleasurable substitute for your attention while he's alone may allay his anxiety. A chew toy or a nylon bone filled with peanut butter or cheese can provide a pleasant pastime for him. But, link this treat to your dog's independence; give it to him only five to ten minutes before you leave.

Some dogs are comforted by household sounds. It may ease your dog's anxiety if you leave a tape recorder running while you're at home, then replay it for him when you are gone. In *The Dog Who Loved Too Much*, Dr. Dodman recounts a client's use of a sound-activated recorder while his dog was alone. Whenever she barked or whined, the dog activated the tape and heard a recording of her owner saying "Lie down, that's a good dog." Though a bit confused at first, the dog quickly learned to follow her owner's command.

While you're treating your dog's separation anxiety, it's important to ban lap time, sleeping on your bed, and to discourage him from following you around the house until the condition has eased. If he does follow you, take him gently to his bed or resting place and command him to go lie down, then praise him for compliance. If your dog is already used to a crate, he may feel more secure inside one while you're away; however, this is not the time to introduce a crate.

INDEPENDENCE TRAINING—"TEACHING YOUR DOG TO STAND ON ITS OWN FOUR FEET"—IS IMPERATIVE FOR SOLVING THE PROBLEM OF SEPARATION ANXIETY.

Medication Treatments

Medication is usually an important component of the successful treatment of separation anxiety. Treating dogs with antidepressants such as Clomicalm and Prozac not only reduces their anxiety, but helps them be more receptive to behavior modification treatment.

According to scientific trials of Clomicalm, the drug is generally well tolerated, although side effects of vomiting, lethargy, and diarrhea did occur in some animals. Be sure to ask your veterinarian about any possible adverse reactions to the drug.

In the past, veterinarians prescribed antidepressants proven effective in humans for dogs with separation anxiety. Amitriptyline (Elavil) was the first anti-depressant used in treating dogs, according to Dr. Dodman. Prozac is another drug originally developed for humans that has crossed over into veterinary use for dogs. These medications also continue to be very effective for treating separation anxiety.

By developing and conducting successful clinical field tests of a drug specifically for dogs, Novartis is a trailblazer, according to Dr. Dodman. He says, "It adds an air of legitimacy to prescribing a drug for separation anxiety. Some vets were nervous about prescribing a human drug for use in dogs."

Another far-reaching benefit is increased awareness of the problem of separation anxiety. Thanks to the availability of medication, dog owners who once believed they had a horrible beast now should understand that, just as in humans, certain mental disorders are common and treatable.

Independence Training Tips

Independence training—"teaching your dog to stand on its own four feet"—is imperative for solving the problem of separation anxiety. Your dog shouldn't demand attention from you; she should get it only when she's calm. Reward positive behavior, not whining or nudging.

Dr. Dodman advises working with your dog daily, training it to obey one word commands, including come, sit, stay, and down-stay. Food can be used as a reward at first, but as the training progresses a pat, an affirmation, or a "good dog" should be sufficient.

Once your dog has learned basic obedience commands, begin training it to down-stay for progressively longer periods. The goal is to achieve a 20 minute down-stay. Start by leading it to a mat or dog bed, rewarding her for every 10 seconds she lies still. Then, increase the time to 20 seconds, 30 seconds, and so on. If it breaks the down-stay, return it to the mat; it will soon learn if it stays, it will get a reward.

When your dog can do a reliable down-stay while you are in the room, begin gradually to distance yourself, first by staying in the room, but occupying yourself with something else, eventually leaving the room. Over time, increase the distance and time you are away until your dog can remain in a down-stay for 30 minutes, even while you are out of the room. ❧

22

Canine Compulsions

*Compulsions are normal behaviors gone awry,
running the gamut from snapping at
imaginary flies to licking paws raw.*

Isn't that cute...the puppy is chasing his tail!" A playful puppy is one thing. But it's an entirely different situation when a dog's tail-chasing is a self-absorbing and even self-injurious activity. Just ask anyone who owns a compulsive tail-chaser.

"Continuous tail chasing is only one of a number of compulsive disorders in which dogs indulge in seemingly pointless, repetitive behaviors," says Dr. Nicholas Dodman, a widely regarded expert on canine compulsions and director of the Tufts Behavior Clinic. Some dogs engage in their particular compulsion—whether it's tail chasing, licking, flank sucking, shadow chasing, fly snapping, spinning or pacing—almost constantly. "They don't eat, they don't sleep. They just spin or lick or pace to the exclusion of everything else," he says, recalling one patient that had worn off the pads from his back feet as a result of his near-constant spinning.

"Whether they're performed by animals or by people, compulsive behaviors are essentially normal instinctive behaviors related to grooming, hunting, movement, and eating—except that they are done repeatedly and out of context," says Dr. Dodman. He is among those researchers, including some at the National Institutes of Health (NIH), who see certain compulsive behaviors in animals as apparent models of similar obsessive-compulsive disorders (OCD) in people, such as hair plucking, excessive hand washing, hoarding, and tics.

It's a sad fact that more than 2.5 million cats and dogs are euthanized annually in the United States because of problem behaviors. Intent on changing that disturbing statistic, Dodman has spent more than a decade studying and treating the spectrum of behavior problems affecting companion animals, including cats, horses, birds and dogs. Overall, he suspects these problems—broadly categorized as aggressions, fears and phobias, and compulsive behaviors—are on the rise. This may be because companion animals are living in increasingly urban and suburban settings that don't fulfill their needs for exercise, environmental stimulation, and human/animal interaction.

By Dr. Dodman's definition, a behavior becomes a compulsion when it is frequent and intense, occupying an hour or more of the dog's day. A behavior may begin quickly or develop over time. Each case varies, and compulsive dogs appear to receive some psychological satisfaction when engaging in the behavior. Although a single specific cause may be impossible to identify, genetic predisposition and environmental stress, and usually, a combination of both, appear related to the development of compulsions. In addition, disorders like tail chasing and fly snapping may be related to mild seizures as well.

However, compulsive canines are now benefiting from innovative treatments that integrate exercise, diet, environmental enrichment, and drug therapy for troublesome behaviors.

Instinctive/Compulsive

■ *Grooming Behaviors/Licking (lick granuloma), scratching, flank sucking, nail chewing*

■ *Hunting Behaviors/Tail chasing, fly snapping, light and shadow chasing*

■ *Movement Behaviors/Pacing, circling, fence walking, digging*

■ *Eating Behaviors/Flank sucking, air licking, rock eating, overeating/drinking*

Common Compulsions

■ Lick Granuloma

It's the "quintessential canine compulsion," Dr. Dodman says, because this excessive grooming behavior was the first compulsive disorder of dogs identified by its similarity to the excessive hand washing of some human OCD patients. Affected dogs intently lick at the wrists of one or both of their front legs or the hocks of their hind legs. They do this to the extent that their skin becomes ulcerated and forms scar tissue (granulation). Excessive scratching, flank sucking and nail chewing are other examples of grooming-based compulsions.

Lick granuloma patients tend to be anxious, sensitive, and highstrung. Some large working and sporting breeds appear to be more genetically predisposed to the problem than other dogs. However, environmental stress contributes to the onset. Susceptible dogs may begin licking as a displacement behavior to relieve their tension, for example, from separation anxiety from its owner, a change in the dog's physical or social environment, or a noise phobia. As the behavior becomes ingrained it continues, even after the initial stress is reduced or removed.

For years, veterinarians tried to prevent dogs from licking by using bandages, salves, and E-collars as barriers to prevent them from reaching their legs. But they had little lasting success. As soon as the E-collar came off, the licking resumed.

■ Tail Chasing and Spinning

At first tail chasing and spinning may sound harmless and even amusing. But, they are canine compulsions that are not just annoying to the owner but potentially injurious to the dog.

Some breeders differentiate between the subtleties of the two activities, but Alice Moon-Fanelli, Ph.D., a behavioral geneticist at Tufts, considers them to be one and the same disorder. Dogs affected by mild tail-chasing may only occasionally chase their tail in response to a specific trigger. Onset is usually gradual, and an owner can easily interrupt the activity.

Moderate to severe tail chasing and spinning may come on quickly or gradually, however, even though there may be no apparent trigger; it can become all-consuming to the point that the canines are unable to function normally.

"Both environmental factors and a dog's genetic background influence the variations in development," says Dr. Moon-Fanelli, whose ongoing study of families of dogs seeks to discover if there is a genetic basis for development of compulsive behaviors, in particular tail chasing and spinning. "The extensive data I've collected on bull terriers suggests the disorder is familial, at least in this breed," Dr. Moon-Fanelli says. Although compulsive tail chasing and spinning can develop in any breed, herding and terrier breeds are most commonly affected.

■ Fly Snapping

Although fly snapping is apparently another displaced predatory or hunting behavior, there may be seizure-related and genetic components as well. Affected dogs stare at invisible insects, snap at the air and their flanks, shake their heads, scratch, and have rapid eye and head movements in the direction of the "attacking flies."

As with other compulsions, there may be some hereditary basis for this less-than-normal activity that occurs in a variety of breeds. If there is seizure activity, the epileptic bouts last a short time. The dog may salivate, defecate and urinate, and then become lethargic or disoriented.

However, for dogs with an apparent compulsive basis for their fly snapping, the bouts are frequent, prolonged and highly disruptive to the dog's once-normal activities.

Similar to other compulsions, such as light and shadow chasing, fly snapping may also evolve into an attention-getting device that's reinforced by the owner's attempts to calm or punish the dog.

Behaviorists have yet to establish certain basic parameters for the disorder, such as the typical age of onset. This is because many owners—who consider fly snapping to be more of an annoyance to them than a danger to their dogs—often don't pursue veterinary treatment for this compulsive behavior.

Treating Compulsions

If you suspect your dog has or is developing a compulsive behavior, first contact your own veterinarian. He or she will want to rule out any medical reason for the behavior. For example, if the dog is constantly licking its leg, it may be affected by an allergy, an injury, parasites, or arthritis. Many veterinarians today have a special interest in animal behavior and are able to diagnose and treat some behavioral disorders at their own practices.

If the behavior proves more challenging, your veterinarian may refer you to either an applied behaviorist or a veterinary behaviorist. Like Dr. Moon-Fanelli, an applied behaviorist is an individual who has a doctoral degree in animal behavior and may also be certified by the Animal Behavior Society. A veterinary behaviorist is a veterinarian who has also completed a residency program in behavior and passed the extensive examinations required to become a specialist as a Diplomate of the American College of Veterinary Behaviorists. Dodman is one of fewer than 25 board-certified veterinary behaviorists. Such specialists are usually affiliated with large veterinary clinics or with teaching hospitals at the nation's 27 veterinary schools and colleges.

If you don't live near a major veterinary facility, don't despair. Many behaviorists make their expertise available through consultations to veterinarians in private practice and to animal owners directly.

When a client brings a dog to Tufts' Behavior Clinic for diagnosis and treatment of a compulsive disorder, Drs. Dodman, Moon-Fanelli and their colleagues take a complete history of the dog's health in order to rule out any medical causes for the behavior and—most important—they take a comprehensive history of the dog's behavior. A behavioral history sometimes turns up the fact that an owner may have unwittingly initiated a compulsion such as light chasing by playing a flashlight game with the dog. But, the dog never stopped playing the game.

"Every case is different, so we ask a lot of questions, looking for the particular 'key' that will unlock a diagnosis and lead to a treatment," Dr. Dodman says. They listen to the owner, and they observe the dog and how it interacts with the owner, evaluating what they see and hear in terms of both the dog's learned and "hard-wired" behaviors.

In developing a plan for treating a canine compulsion, some of the approaches Drs. Dodman and Moon-Fanelli may consider range from environmental to behavioral to pharmacological:

Tools for Treatment

Successfully treating compulsive behavior in dogs requires cooperation between owner and veterinarian. Your dog's medical and emotional history is one of your veterinarian's most useful diagnostic and treatment tools. Here's what you can do to compile a history:

■ Find out if your dog's siblings or parents exhibit compulsive behavior.

■ Keep a written record of your dog's daily activities. Note how long compulsive behavior lasts, how frequently it occurs, and exactly

what it looks like. Note whether your dog exhibits certain behaviors at specific times or after particular events.
■ Video- or audiotape your dog's behavior.
■ List results of any previous diagnostic tests and detail any prior attempts at treatment.

TREATMENT PLANS CAN RANGE FROM
ENVIRONMENTAL TO BEHAVIORAL TO
PHARMACOLOGICAL

Developing a Treatment Plan

■ Identification of the Conflict
What stresses trigger a dog's behavior? Mealtime? The owner leaving for work? Once the stress is identified, you'll want to eliminate or desensitize the dog to the event.

■ Environmental Enrichment
Think of it as canine occupational therapy. Dogs need activities that fulfill their innate behavioral needs. For example, a herding dog needs balls and other toys to round up and roll around the house or yard. Don't forget that dogs are social animals that enjoy the companionship of "their" people and other dogs.

■ Exercise
Become your dog's personal trainer, joining him for a brisk walk or a game of fetch. There's a lot of truth in the old adage that "a tired dog is a good dog."

■ Diet
Feed a diet that's appropriate to a dog's activities. A lapdog doesn't need to eat "high-octane" rations better suited to active sporting dogs. In fact, Dr. Moon-Fanelli is conducting a study to find out if compulsive behaviors can be reduced by feeding low-protein diets.

■ Daily Structure

Just as young children thrive on a daily schedule, dogs too feel more se-cure—and less anxious—when there is a predictable routine to the day.

■ Attention Withdrawal

Turn a cold shoulder to a dog's compulsive behavior—unless, of course, it's in danger of injury. A dog picks up on subtle cues from its owners, so it's best to ignore a dog when it is so engaged.

■ Eliminate Discipline

Once a compulsion is established, disciplining the dog is ineffec-tive because the dog isn't able to control its behavior. Discipline may increase a dog's anxiety or reinforce an attention-getting behavior.

■ Obedience Training

As the tune goes "...accentuate the positive, eliminate the negative..." You've worked hard to eliminate negative influences, so now use obedience training to accentuate positive behavior. If you're not fa-miliar with basic obedience training, ask your veterinarian to rec-ommend a good trainer who uses gentle techniques.

■ Counterconditioning

Practice a program of counter-conditioning to interrupt unwanted behavior by training the dog to respond to a command, such as "sit-stay," that's incompatible with its compulsion to spin, for example.

■ Pharmacological Therapy

When a compulsive behavior is deeply ingrained, all your efforts to remove the cause of conflict and follow the steps of the treatment program simply may not be enough. Fortunately, veterinarians and veterinary behaviorists can prescribe any of several antidepressant medications. These are used with similar disorders in people and are also available for treating compulsive behaviors in dogs and other animals. Two of these familiar drugs are fluoxetine (Prozac) and clomipramine (Anafranil, Clomi-calm).

A pioneer in veterinary pharmacological therapy, Dr. Dodman thinks of these therapies as behavioral tools that are best suited for short-term use. Although it can take several weeks for them to begin taking effect, these drugs are used successfully to help calm an anx-ious pet and make it more receptive to your important behavior mod-ification, environmental enrichment, and counterconditioning techniques. ❖

23

Attention-Getting Behavior

The objective in treating attention-getting behavior is to curtail or extinguish the behavior, primarily by cutting off all reinforcement of it.

Many of us find it endearing when our dogs nuzzle us with their heads, drop balls at our feet, prance around with food dishes in their mouths, or paw aside the newspaper we're reading. The messages are clear: "Pat me!" "Play with me!" "Feed me!" "Pay attention to me!"

It's natural for dogs to want our attention. As pack animals, they thrive on "social" interaction, especially with the person (or canine) "in charge." In wolf packs, lower-ranking pack members solicit attention from—and display affection for—dominant members. Similarly, companionable family dogs tend to focus their interest on people.

Dogs are very careful observers of human behavior, and "they learn quickly what gets their owners' attention," says Dr. Nicholas Dodman. Although dogs may not have the problem-solving capacity to devise plots for snaring our attention, trial and error seems to work well enough. Using this method, dogs discover what succeeds and use these successful techniques again and again.

Whether it's a wagging tail, a plaintive whine, or a paw on the knee, most attention-getting behavior in dogs is simply an attempt at social interaction. As long as this social behavior doesn't bother you, your family, or visitors, there's probably no cause for concern.

Crossing the Line

Like other "normal" canine behaviors, attention-getting behavior sometimes crosses the line from engaging to problematic. Owners often start complaining when an acceptable behavior (like scratching at the carpet) shifts to an unacceptable one (like eating the carpet) or when the intensity or frequency of a behavior markedly increases.

"Problem" attention-getters may chronically whine or bark, pester with snout or paw, damage household property, injure themselves (self-mutilation), chase their tails or invisible shadows, or even feign lameness.

Despite wide variability in attention-getting behavior, there is one common denominator: the dog's actions earn it extra attention from people. The whiner gets petted; the dog that stands in front of the TV is moved aside (verbally or physically); and the dog that engages in more bizarre behavior—such as shadow-chasing—becomes the focus of its owner's perplexed attention.

Likely Candidates

No one has conclusively determined what role, if any, heredity plays in the development of attention-getting behavior. Anecdotal observations suggest that certain breeds (golden retrievers and Boston terriers among them) seem to have a greater need to be held, petted, and entertained. But no genetic studies have been done to confirm these observations.

One thing is certain: a dog's early experiences and its relationships with owner and family can establish the foundation for problematic attention-seeking behavior. For example, canine fear and insecurity arising from early abuse, neglect, or inadequate socialization are sometimes the root cause of a dog's constant wheedling for human attention.

But problematic attention seeking usually doesn't occur without significant (though often unwitting) human encouragement. "Owners who insist on attending to their dog's every whim often make the rod for their own backs," points out Dr. Dodman. "'Matter-offactish" owners are less likely to encounter this problem."

Sometimes, this problem behavior can arise from a change in a dog's environment. Attention-getting behavior sometimes begins when a new baby enters the scene. (Warning: Don't confuse aggression—growling, snapping, or biting—directed at the baby with attention-seeking behavior. Aggression has different behavioral origins and calls for a different treatment approach.) Expectant parents must prepare their dog in advance for Junior's arrival. (Despite the undeniable excitement that comes along with a new infant, owners must make sure they set aside time after the baby's arrival for their dog's social and exercise needs.

Multidog households can also be a "breeding ground" for attention-getting behavior, as pooches vie for access to human family members. But in some multidog households, attention getting is virtually nonexistent because dogs manage to meet the social demands of one another. In a few multidog households, dogs have even been known to use a fellow canine's attention-getting behavior to their own advantage.

WHICHEVER CORRECTIVE TECHNIQUE YOU AND YOUR VETERINARIAN SELECT, ALWAYS RESPOND TO INAPPROPRIATE BEHAVIOR WITH YOUR CHOSEN METHOD.

Don't Jump to Conclusions

Before attempting to treat problem attention-getting behavior, always have your veterinarian first rule out underlying medical conditions that could cause such conduct. "Sometimes—especially in older dogs—underlying medical problems intensify a dog's attention-seeking behavior," notes Dr. Dodman. A painful condition, in particular, may prompt a dog of any age to solicit extra attention from its owner. In such cases, once veterinary treatment addresses the dog's pain, the attention-getting behavior usually disappears.

Proper Reinforcement

The objective in treating attention-getting behavior is to curtail or extinguish the behavior—primarily by cutting off all reinforcement of it. At the same time, an owner must consistently reward desirable behavior—no matter how mundane—with praise, petting, or treats. "Praise your dog even if it's just lying quietly in its bed," recommends Dr. Dodman. "It will then learn that you approve of its being calm."

The simplest—but not necessarily most effective—way to curb canine attention-getting behavior is to ignore your dog when it "begs" for attention. A more proactive technique—withdrawing attention from your dog—may hasten the process. For example, walk away from your dog whenever it displays the undesirable behavior. If you do this consistently, Bowser will soon understand that the actions that once attracted your attention now cause you to leave—the exact opposite of what he wants. (Here, attention withdrawal works as negative reinforcement—something your dog wants to avoid.)

To boost the learning value of attention withdrawal, some behaviorists recommend that you immediately precede your withdrawal with an audible signal—such as a duck call or whistle. This technique helps your dog associate the withdrawal of attention with another distinct event, which reinforces the connection between its behavior and your withdrawal response.

As a last resort in hard-to-manage cases, some behaviorists recommend pain-free punishment applied from a distance. (Punishment, as defined by animal behaviorists, is the application of an undesirable stimulus after a misbehavior. One potential drawback: punishment sometimes increases anxiety in an already nervous dog.) The most common—and humane—form of punishment is to judiciously squirt the misbehaving dog with a water-filled spray bottle. It helps to have an "accomplice" with you to carry out this technique. As soon as your dog begins agitating for attention, your cohort surreptitiously sprays it with water. Most dogs don't like the sensation, especially when the squirt seems to come out of nowhere.

Although it might seem a common-sense approach to curbing attention-getting behavior, a verbal reprimand is actually counterproductive. Harsh words are likely to reinforce rather than extinguish the behavior. If your pooch's attention-seeking behavior is mildly annoying rather than totally nerve-wracking, you might want to consider a "learn to earn" or "no free lunch" approach. When your dog comes looking for attention, tell it firmly but pleasantly to sit or lie down. Never reward the dog (with attention or anything else) until it obeys. If necessary, repeat the exercise several times until the pestering ceases. Many attention-seeking dogs actually enjoy interacting with their owners through command-and-obey exercises like this. It's a true win-win situation.

Whichever corrective technique you and your veterinarian select, always respond to inappropriate behavior with your chosen method. If you "slip up" even occasionally, the intermittent reinforcement serves to sustain the behavior you're trying to eliminate. Also, in the interest of consistency, always reward good behavior.

Even Negative Attention...

Believe it or not, when your dog demands attention, it may not be looking for affection. "Some dogs perceive any kind of attention, good or bad, as a reward," says Dr. Nicholas Dodman. Ironically, your sharp admonitions—"Stop that!" or "Be quiet!"—may actually encourage your dog to continue pestering because your dog views the reprimand as a reward.

Owners may have an overriding urge to reprimand seemingly "mindless" attention-getting behaviors such as tail-chasing (which often begin as anxiety-reducing behaviors). But owners actually reinforce such annoying behavior with loud and repeated "cease and desist" commands. The real danger is that the continual reinforcement these reprimands give your dog may make its attention-getting behavior become compulsive .

Preventive "Medicine"

Prevention is always preferable to treatment. And this adage certainly applies to attention getting and other canine behavior problems. "To prevent attention-getting behavior, develop a healthy lifestyle for you and your dog," suggests Dr. Dodman. This could include teaming up with your dog for basic obedience training, providing lots of interactive exercise (ball or stick fetching, for example), or acclimating your dog to spending more time alone.

Remember, you need not disrupt the loving relationship between you and your dog as you work to prevent or curtail unwanted attention-getting behavior. Use attention withdrawal only for the specific behavior you're trying to eliminate. As you know, there are many times when your dog legitimately needs—and deserves—your attention.

One of our hard-working dog consultants regularly takes advantage of her canine housemate's nearly unquenchable thirst for human attention. When the attention-seeker is sacked out in the much-coveted dog nest, our shrewd consultant grabs a fleece toy and shakes it vigorously. This, of course, gets the attention of her well-trained owners, who stop what they're doing to play with her. The "jealous" sister invariably bolts out of bed, insisting on her share of the action. The crafty canine with the ulterior motive then scampers into the empty (but warm) nest. The moral of the story: despite one dog hoodwinking the other, both get what they want, and no harm is done. ❁

24

Scoop on Housesoiling

Some breeds are typically harder to housetrain than others and may require an extra measure of patience and vigilance.

One reason dogs are considered "easy" pets is because you can easily train them to use the great outdoors as their "bathroom." Nevertheless, housesoiling does create problems for many owners. In fact, housesoiling—repeated urination and defecation indoors by a dog old enough to know better—accounts for 20 percent of the problems animal behaviorists see. Dogs that are chronic housesoilers often end up at shelters—or worse, euthanized. But with a little professional help, owners can resolve most housesoiling problems.

Dogs are generally clean animals. In fact, mothers of wild canids ingest the waste produced by their young to prevent parasites from infesting the den. By 7 or 8 weeks of age, though, a puppy's hygiene instincts kick in, and it begins to eliminate away from its sleeping area. Many owners capitalize on this developing fastidiousness by using crates as housetraining tools

You'll be most successful with housetraining if you schedule your dog's outdoor "potty" trips and positively reinforce outdoor elimination habits. One rule of thumb: a young puppy can "hold it" for the number of hours equal to its age in months plus one. For example, a 2-month-old should be able to last for 3 hours—give or take. As your pup shows increasing control, gradually stretch out the time between outdoor bathroom breaks.

For punishment to be effective, it must immediately follow the undesirable behavior. Consequently, it's pointless to punish your dog when you find evidence of an "accident" that's already taken place. But if you catch your pup "in the act," interrupt it with a startling noise such as a hand clap or a quick squirt from a water bottle. (Harsh punishment may discourage your pup from eliminating at all when you're present—even outdoors.) About 30 seconds after interrupting your dog, take it outside to finish its "business"—and praise it lavishly for doing so. Always make sure to clean and deodorize the scene of every indoor accident to eradicate the olfactory triggers that prompt dogs to go again in the same place.

When selecting a dog, keep in mind some breeds—especially those traditionally housed in kennels—are typically harder to housetrain than others and may require an extra measure of patience and vigilance. Another note: females are usually easier to housetrain than males.

"Refresher" Course

If your dog's housesoiling stems from incomplete house-training, you might try some remedial training:

■ *Keep your dog confined in a comfortable crate when you can't supervise it.*

■ *Escort the dog to the same outdoor location every 3 hours (familiar smells stimulate elimination) and soon after it eats, naps, or plays. Give the dog 3 to 4 minutes to take care of its business. Use verbal encouragement such as "do your stuff."*

■ *When your dog "does its stuff," immediately lavish it with praise; then bring it inside and give it a small food treat.*

■ *If your dog doesn't "go" outdoors during the allotted time, bring it indoors for 15 minutes; then return to the appointed spot and try again.*

Why Housesoiling?

If your previously well-housetrained dog has begun housesoiling, enlist your veterinarian to investigate possible medical causes. For example, both Cushing's disease and diabetes mellitus (and even some prescription drugs) can undermine bladder and bowel control. It is utterly ineffective and unfair to your dog to treat medical incontinence (loss of control over elimination) as a behavior problem.

If your veterinarian rules out medical causes, you should look to behavioral causes. "The most common nonmedical reason for housesoiling is improper housetraining," explains Dr. Jean DeNapoli, a resident at the Behavior Clinic at Tufts University School of Veterinary Medicine. "People sometimes stop housetraining too soon, assuming the pup has everything under control." Unfortunately, rehousetraining requires more dogged determination than doing it right the first time.

Housetraining efforts can also unravel as the weather turns cold. Some dogs are reluctant to do their business outside in the cold. (Try a doggie sweater!) And some owners—looking ruefully at the bitter-cold darkness outside—think wishfully (but mistakenly) that their young puppy can wait until morning.

Other common behavioral reasons for housesoiling are extreme submissiveness, indoor territorial marking, and separation anxiety (see illustrations). Effectively treating these problems means "understanding your dog's view of the world and consistently following the treatment plan," advises Dennis Fetko, Ph.D., an applied animal behaviorist from San Diego.

■ Submissive Urination

A sign of deference toward a "dominant" person or dog, this occurs most often in young female dogs. If you see this behavior pattern developing, try to close the "dominance gap." "De-dominate" your own body language by crouching down, averting your eyes, and speaking softly when your dog approaches you. Show affection with chest scratches rather than head pats. You might also boost your submissive dog's confidence by letting it prevail at games like "keep away."

■ Neutering

Male dogs have a hormone-driven penchant for territorial marking and leave urinary "calling cards" outdoors. But unneutered males may exhibit this behavior indoors as well—especially when under the social duress of having a "new" human or canine housemate arrive or a neighborhood female dog go into heat.

Castration stops indoor urine marking almost 90 percent of the time. But as added insurance, some people cordon off favorite indoor marking spots or make them undesirable. You may also want to consider antianxiety medication (available by prescription only).

■ Separation Anxiety

Dogs with separation anxiety are so attached to their owners that they become extremely agitated when left alone and may lose bladder and/or bowel control. Such dogs do not soil the house to get back at their owner for leaving. They simply can't help themselves. If an owner responds to this type of housesoiling with punishment, the already anxious dog will become even more anxious, more eager to please, and increasingly dependent on its owner.

Experts recommend desensitizing an anxious housesoiler by ignoring it when you arrive and depart. Reward it for staying calm during gradually lengthening periods of solitude. Also, exercise your dog briskly before leaving it alone; enrich your dog's environment with stimulating toys and "sustained release" food treats; and, if necessary, ask your veterinarian about antianxiety medication.

Owners are sometimes bewildered by the many possible causes of housesoiling—both medical and behavioral. But with a modicum of patience and persistence, you should be able to solve your dog's housesoiling problems. ❖

25

Barking Around the Clock

Barking is typically a symptom of an unsatisfied need; determining the cause is the owner's first major challenge.

Though we don't have the sirens of city streets and bustling sounds of urban congestion, the air in our Rocky Mountain neighborhood is continuously filled with its own orchestra and chorus.

Shortly after sundown during winter months the arrival of stars is usually accompanied by the yapping of a pack of coyotes celebrating the arrival of darkness. Those are the sounds of the wild.

Similarly, when animal trainer Troy Hyde, who lives a quarter-mile up the road, serves breakfast to his pack of wolves, he is always greeted by howling that echoes the length of the valley. That's romantic.

There is nothing symphonic or artistic about the howling that emanates from the 14 dogs who live at the neighboring Black Dog Ranch when they greet the mailman, delivery vans, or newsboy, though. Their barking is just noise.

The same holds true for our dogs, Blondie the Lab and Cody the mutt. Blondie thinks it's her responsibility to protect the neighborhood from intruders, so will stake out a position on the hillside and greet school buses, snow plows, and the FedEx driver with a throaty howl.

Cody's racket is more civilized but may be equally annoying: the Samoyed blood coursing through his veins produces a chatterbox effect. He typically greets the day, his owners, and visitors with a raucous, high pitched 'howdy.' It's cute, most of the time.

Since the general attitude in the mountains is "if you don't like dogs barking, move," the most neighborly approach is to ignore the racket. Unfortunately, that's not an option for many in urban areas, where nuisance barking often leads to acrimonious relations with the neighbors, frustrated attempts by owners to stifle their dogs' barking, and, all too often, a decision to give up the dog.

"We trained several dogs in mid-town Manhattan which, had their barking continued, would have been left for adoption or their owners evicted by irate landlords," says SarahWilson, co-author with Brian Kilcommons of *Good Owners, Great Dogs*.

Though our circumstances are less dramatic, we remain unconvinced that barking is a condition we must endure—which equates to surrendering to the dogs' misbehavior—so embarked on a journey that we hoped would lead to peace and quiet.

Why Dogs Bark

In order to curtail problem barking, it's helpful to determine why your dog is barking. Like most dog behavior, barking is typically a symptom of an **unsatisfied need**, so determining the cause from a laundry list of possibilities becomes an owner's first major challenge.

Barking is simply a dog's means of communication, whether directed at other dogs, at members of the household, or at the world in general. It may be an attempt to **stake out territory**, or **warn owners of intruders**. Since dogs are social animals, it could be a symptom of **loneliness** and attempt to get attention—announcing to the unseen but very audible early-morning chorus of his peers that, "Yeah, I'm here too!" A lack of exercise and interaction with humans, or other dogs, may produce barking, as will **boredom** when left alone indoors for extended periods of time.

In a worst-case scenario, a pet may suffer from separation-anxiety syndrome and bark continuously when left alone. Or barking can denote other forms of distress, including **chronic pain**.

Sarah Wilson sums up: "They hear a noise; they're lonely; they want your attention; they're having fun; they're frightened, or their toy has run under the couch," she says. "It's their way of letting us know they need or want something, or can be a warning that something is not right."

Controlled barking in response to those types of stimuli, like Cody's jabbering, is a far cry from **chronic barking** that may result in a dog's relocation. Even a "good dog" will bark too much occasionally or inappropriately—behavior that can be dealt with the same way as any other quirks that appear from time-to-time: Ignore, don't reward the behavior, then reinforce the desired behavior (quiet) positively. Incessant problem barking may require more concentrated training. But even the most troublesome cases tend to respond to thoughtful and thorough training or re-training.

The first step to solving that problem may be hiring a trainer to evaluate the dog and it's environment. "Our first considerations are whether the dog's needs are being met. Does it have a proper diet? Is the owner providing leadership and structure? Is it in good health and receiving adequate exercise?" Wilson said.

"Training may begin by introducing distractions—telling the dog to 'sit' when it barks, for example," she said. "Do a two-minute drill with a command he knows, like 'down,' which is especially effective since it's harder to bark when he's laying down."

Yelling has proven ineffective, especially when it occurs after the event. "Yelling at a barking dog may sound to the dog like you're just joining in the fun," Kilcommons says. The same holds true for spraying with a hose or hitting him with a beanbag—although some trainers feel a distraction, such as a shake-can or tossed newspaper, works well as an interruption.

Martin R Smith, DVM of Drs. Foster and Smith, which markets pets products, says training starts at puppyhood. "If you have a barking puppy the best advice is to ignore the behavior. You're simply not encouraging the undesirable behavior," Martin says.

"Some dogs bark out of sheer boredom. Make sure she has toys to play with and a bone or chew treat to keep her occupied. Don't leave her caged or outdoors for extended periods of time. They are social animals and need attention."

Well-adjusted dogs may bark if they can't see what's going on in the world around them—who or what is making a noise. If provided a view of the street—from house or yard—those ominous footsteps may be indentified with the kids down the street, a slamming car door with the neighbor arriving home. Once identified, the stimulation is no longer a threat.

Some dogs with severe separation anxiety may require more extensive professional evaluation and training, possibly even some calming medication in the meantime.

What To Do

■ Reward Training

Trainer and author Ian Dunbar, DVM offers several methods for controlling barking. One is a variation on simple diversion and is especially helpful for dogs who bark or otherwise act up when lonely or bored. He recommends that chew toys filled with pet food or other treats should be left when the owner expects to be away. You can use a Kong or hollow sterilized bone stuffed with a variety of fillings—honey and kibble, peanut butter, yoghurt—whatever your dog likes. In summer months, the toys can be chilled in the freezer to create frozen treats.

"It's a proven fact that a dog can't bark and chew at the same time, and you give him something to do for extended periods of time," Dr. Dunbar says.

Reward training, especially useful at defusing such situations as a knock on the door, involves exposing the dog to the situation (with the help of a friend who plays the doorbell-ringer) and gradually getting the dog to break off barking at a certain point (many owners want their dogs to sound a brief alert at strangers/guests on the property). Rewarding the dog when he does quiet down—with praise and what Dunbar calls a "shush cookie," eventually will win dogs over.

Reward training is the best way to go and produces desired reults in at least 85 percent of behavior cases, says Dr. Nicholas Dodman. Older notions of training, based on punishment or negative reinforcement, are intended to get a dog to stop doing something, he said.

Left, Trainer Ian Dunbar, kibble reward hidden in hand, requests Oso to "Speak!" Right, Oso complies with Dunbar's command to "Shush!" Dunbar uses both verbal and hand cues.

Reward-based training is designed to encourage a dog to do something. "The opposite of reward is not punishment—it's no reward."

■ Lure/Reward Training

In a slightly more advanced method, similar to Wilson's "stimulating barking," Dunbar advises owners who enjoy a good relationship with their animal to try lure/reward training. This involves training your dog to speak on cue, giving you a measure of control over the barking, which is, after all, he says, "normal dog behavior." You can practice this again with someone at the door in the following sequence: 'Speak,' Ring, Bark, 'Shush,' reward.

"If you put a behavior problem on cue, it becomes an obedience response," Dunbar says. It gives you the control over when, and to what extent, your dog barks.

We've experimented with several of these techniques, with some success; at this point, Cody needs more training but at least he's now talking from a sitting position.

Anti-barking Devices

When basic training methods fail to change a dog's behavior many pet owners turn in desperation to some of the new, artificial devices intended to solve the barking problem.

These aversive devices come in several iterations: free-standing units or collars that emit a harsh, audible tone; voice-activated collars that broadcast a citronella spray; and collars with contact points that transmit an electronic shock to the dog. Generally, we think these are a poor substitute for continued training.

■ Audible Devices

The least objectionable of what Dunbar calls "gizmos," are, in our opnion, the audible devices that operate on a premise that a distraction—in this case an obnoxious sound—occurring at the time a dog barks will result in cessation of that behavior. We saw the best and worst results they may produce.

Amtek Pet Behavior Products, which has marketed audible units since 1986, sells three types of 'Barker Breaker' devices. They emit a tone that reaches 112 decibels when within 10 feet of the pet, well above conversational tones.

The unit we tested, the Super Barker Breaker, is activated when the owner pushes a button on top of the case, which fits in the palm of a hand. In order to inhibit barking with this method, the owner must continually be in the presence of the dog, and activate the unit each time he barks; that's a tall order.

As an alternative, the unit may be left in auto mode to be activated when the dog barks within 25 feet of the microphone. The microphone's sensitivity level is adjusted by rotating a knob on top of the unit.

In our outdoor tests we learned that, to be effective, the sensitivity level was set so high that other sounds set off the device. In an urban setting, that could be as troublesome as barking. At lower sensitivity levels, the dog must bark directly into the microphone, which presents a challenging training opportunity.

When Blondie is in guard-dog mode she is assiduous about announcing the arrival of the FedEx driver, which is enough of an annoyance and distraction that we tested the unit indoors by setting it next to the entry. In the process, we learned that there's a thin line between pet correction and sensory overload.

After setting of the alarm several times, Blondie only barked once, heard the tone, and quieted. However, when she and Cody entered the house together and he announced his presence with a high pitched yip, the alarm sounded. He was undeterred, but Blondie and her fragile psyche beat a path upstairs, acting as though she'd been punished unjustly. It took two days for her to remove the hang-dog expression from her face.

The tone emitted by these devices is as annoying to humans as to the dog. It's clearly not indicated in confined living spaces, such as an apartment building, or when there are people in the household trying to sleep. Another serious drawback is that these devices can be set off by a second dog, which is why we don't care for the collar version.

■ Citronella

The citronella correction method, the latest product to hit the American market, has been used extensively in Europe and Australia for 15 years. Here's how it works: A collar with sensor with a microphone is attached to the dog's neck, and the sensor is filled with citronella from a pressurized can. When the dog barks the microphone picks up the sound and the unit emits spray under the dog's nose.

The principle underlying the operation of this collar is that a blast of spray will cause the dog to hear, see, and smell the spray and thus be distracted from barking since a dog's olfactories are many times more sensitive than a human's. Citronella is the scent of choice since it is a non-toxic Asiatic grass that yields an oil that smells like lemon.

This is the product of choice for many because it is perceived as being more humane than a shock collar. However, it shares the drawback that it can be set off by another dog, and can make some dogs sick while not deterring others. "In our experience, dogs can learn to adjust the collar, and to empty the cannisters," Wilson says.

Consumers will discover that this is the most expensive of artificial devices we evaluated: at the time we tested it, Radio Systems Spray Control cost $149, which includes a cannister that produces 15-20 sprays. Considering the (then) $15 cost for refills, and the dog's potential ability to defeat the system, the price can add up quickly. We'd liken the spray to Mace-ing a dog and don't like it on the principle that aversion therapy is the evil flip side of reward-based training.

∎ Electric Shock Collars
Don't like them, don't believe in them, would never use one on our dogs, an opinion shared by Drs. Dunbar and Dodman. When are electric shock collars appropriate as anti-barking or behavior training devices? "Never," says Dodman. ❧

26

My Turf

If you understand how dogs perceive territory, you can learn to prevent, or at least curtail, unwanted territorial behavior in your dog.

Kepa sounds the alert—a vigorous "ruff, ruff, ruff"—as the letter carrier comes up the walk. Jill, Kepa's person, usually appreciates advance notice when someone is approaching. But when Jill sees that the object of Kepa's attention is a postal worker, she tells Kepa it's "OK," and the dog immediately settles down.

Next door to Kepa lives Ginger. Ginger barks incessantly and lunges with bared teeth at the letter carrier (and just about anyone else who approaches the property). Ginger's owner, Jack, can barely restrain Ginger, despite repeated attempts to calm her down.

Both dogs are exhibiting forms of territorial behavior—protecting their space against intruders. But while Kepa's barking is a welcome warning, Ginger's behavior is inappropriate for the circumstances—and potentially dangerous.

Like many other instinctive canine behaviors, territorial behavior can become inappropriately intense. It can escalate into excessive barking, urine marking inside the house, and indiscriminate attacks on visitors (both two- and four-legged). But if you understand how dogs perceive territory, you can learn to prevent—or at least curtail—unwanted territorial behavior in your dog.

What Is Territory?

Defining and protecting territory is crucial to the survival of wolves, our dogs' forebears. Wolf packs stake territorial claims to ensure access to necessary resources such as food and dens. Wolves urine-mark conspicuous objects within their territory—olfactory "no trespassing" signs that neighboring wolves recognize and generally respect. If an intruder "steps over the line," wolves in the resident pack vigorously defend their territory.

Domesticated dogs typically define their "turf" as the house and yard. "But a dog's concept of territory doesn't necessarily end at the fence posts," says Dr. Nicholas Dodman. "Some dogs consider any areas they have marked with urine as theirs." For example, if your dog marks the route of your nightly walk, it may view the whole block as home turf, challenging any dogs that invade the space. Territorial behavior usually intensifies as a dog nears its own yard and house, which represent den, dinner, and security. (On the other hand, dogs that fiercely defend their own turf are often very friendly when on "neutral" ground.)

Territorial Responses

Dogs send out "keep out" signals to avoid physical altercations. A dog delivers "no trespassing" messages to other dogs by repeated urine markings around the perimeter of its house or yard. Some highly territorial dogs—primarily intact males—also urine-mark inside the house. This troublesome behavior may be curtailed by neutering.

When a highly territorial dog spies someone or something unfamiliar on its turf, it typically barks while staring down the intruder and raising its hackles (piloerection). For most territorial dogs, that's as far as it goes. Some, however, cross over into uncontrollable barking and more threatening behaviors, such as growling, chasing, and biting. If you encounter such a dog, it's best to avoid eye contact.

Genes and Learning

The instinct for territorial behavior is part of a normal dog's genetic endowment. An overbearing territorial response may be, in part, a manifestation of a dog's inherent dominance, while a weaker response may indicate a more submissive nature. But the frequency and intensity of territorial behavior can be altered through learning.

Over the years, people have selectively bred certain types of dogs to guard hearth, home, and farm. Dogs ranging in size from rottweilers and akitas to dachshunds and fox terriers are genetically predisposed to heightened territoriality, with males more likely than females to display the behavior. But individual dogs within a breed—and even within specific bloodlines—show significant variations in territorial behavior. In fact, some dogs that belong to supposedly ultraterritorial breeds eagerly share their space with other dogs and people.

Here's a classic example of territorial behavior reinforced through learning: a letter carrier approaches the house and is greeted by a wildly barking dog. The letter carrier quickly deposits the mail and continues his or her rounds. The dog is then convinced that its barking scared away the intruder, emboldening it to chase and bite in the future. (Last year, U.S. letter carriers reported more than 2,700 dog-bite incidents.)

Territorial behavior that begins with fear can also be reinforced through learning. For example, a young, naturally shy dog that is afraid of strangers may bark in response to a knock at the door. If the dog's owners repeatedly praise it for barking and if visitors are put off, the owners have laid the groundwork for increasing territoriality. "What's genetic is the timidity, and what's learned is the form of the response," explains Dr. Dodman. To avoid reinforcing extreme territoriality, owners should make early socialization a priority.

Toning It Down

■ Obedience Training

The good news is that you can overcome many of the problems associated with territorial behavior. Basic obedience training helps form a solid foundation for behavior-modification techniques that can defuse aggressive territoriality. If your dog charges at passersby or leaps at visitors, keep it on a lead, teach it the "sit-stay" command, and employ the command (with an appropriate reward) before the dog starts to act out. Consistently using these obedience techniques protects the innocent and reminds your dog that you're in charge.

■ Behavior Modification

Once you've trained your dog in basic obedience, consistently applying behavior-modification techniques can help your dog "unlearn" undesirable territorial behavior. As with many other canine behavior problems, the two main approaches for remedying overzealous territorial responses are systematic **desensitization** and **counterconditioning**. (Owners who simply shout "No!" or forcefully punish a dog are inviting the dog to redirect aggression toward them.)

■ Desensitization

To desensitize your dog, you have to expose it to small doses of the stimulus that triggers its territorial defense and then gradually increase the intensity of the stimulus over time. Always reward your dog for good behavior and do not proceed too quickly to the next level of intensity lest you incite a full-fledged territorial response.

■ Counterconditioning

You also want your dog to view visitors as the source of positive "vibes." Herein lies the crux of counterconditioning: your dog learns to anticipate feeling good in situations that formerly caused upset. Supply your friends with dog treats and arrange for them to visit (individually at first, and then in small groups). If Rover sits and stays rather than lunges, your guests should give him a treat. Throughout the visit, your guests may casually flick treats in Rover's direction—as long as he's staying quiet. After several such controlled experiences with various people, Rover will begin to treat visitors like guests rather than invaders. (In Wales, meter readers carry rubber balls and dog biscuits to ward off attacks from territorial pets.)

Used in tandem, desensitization and counterconditioning are highly effective. But the techniques require time (up to 3 or 4 months) and patience to work. To increase the odds of success, consult an experienced animal behaviorist. You can also boost the effectiveness of the techniques with some basic canine lifestyle changes, including a lower-energy diet and increased daily exercise. (Make sure you consult your veterinarian about these changes and gradually implement them.) Also, veterinarian-prescribed medications such as beta blockers—chemicals that reduce heart rate, blood pressure, and overall anxiety—can accelerate the learning process.

An Ounce of Prevention

Preventing behavior problems is easier than treating them after they develop. Although you can't predict a young puppy's odds of becoming excessively territorial (the behavior doesn't show up until puberty), you can try to avert excessive displays of territorial behavior through socialization both during and after puppyhood.

Expose your puppy to as many different people as possible. Greet neighbors when you're in the yard or taking your pup for a walk, and encourage them to gently pet your dog. Invite people to your home for "puppy parties" during which friends and relatives get to play with the dog and perhaps offer food treats. Your dog will quickly learn to associate new people with pleasant experiences and sensations.

"I think dogs should perceive everyone who approaches them as a friend—until proven otherwise," says Suzanne Hetts, Ph.D., a certified animal behaviorist in Littleton, Colorado. "Helping your dog adopt a friendly, outgoing attitude won't diminish its natural wariness in dangerous situations. Dogs can sense when somebody isn't supposed to be around just by the way people approach and move."

No Mixed Messages

If you don't know how territorial you want your dog to be, you can bet that Rover is confused, too. What's a dog to think when its people encourage hyperalertness and then reprimand it when it displays territorial aggression? "People who want a dog specifically for protection but also want a dog that doesn't bark much or get territorially aggressive are asking a lot from a dog," cautions John Wright, an animal behaviorist and adjunct faculty member at the University of Georgia School of Veterinary Medicine.

Many home-security specialists believe that the mere presence of a dog on your property is a deterrent to would-be intruders. "A moderate-sized dog with a good bark is usually ample warning," agrees Professor Wright.

Ultimately, you're better off treating your dog as a loving member of your family rather than a home-security device. The healthier the bond you establish, the more likely your dog will intuitively (and appropriately) know when to protect you and your home. But you have to teach your dog where the boundary lines of appropriate behavior lie—and help your dog stay on the right side of them. ❧

27

Faces of Aggression

Inappropriate aggression, while occasionally a result of medical disorders, is more commonly caused by human mismanagement.

On the surface, it's easy to distinguish an aggressive dog from a friendly one. Aggressive dogs bark, growl, snap, and bite, sometimes launching assaults that result in serious injury—even death—to humans and other animals. But the broad term "aggression" embraces various biological factors and motivations that make aggression multidimensional and complex. Under-standing aggression better may help you recognize early-warning signs and possibly avoid dangerous mishaps.

We can compare canine aggression to Cerberus, the mythological three-headed dog that guarded the Underworld. One aspect of aggression is its usefulness as a canine survival tool. Another is its usefulness to humans. People have channeled natural canine aggression into helpful behaviors that safeguard families and property. But people have also helped to create the third aspect of aggression—the aspect that is annoying, at best, and dangerous at worst.

Inherited Trait

Dogs inherited the potential for aggressive behavior from their canine cousin, the wolf. Aggressive behavior helps wolves survive in the wild. (After all, a meat eater without the drive to capture and kill prey is doomed to a short and hungry life.) Moreover, wolves, as social animals, must establish a "pack hierarchy," and they do so using aggressive displays. Demonstrative (but usually harmless) skirmishes help establish each member's position in the hierarchy, which leads eventually to coordinated group activity that benefits the entire pack. The pack's desire to protect its young and defend its territory can also lead to aggressive behavior.

As pack animals, dogs are naturally well-suited to join human groups and accept human leadership. Long ago, we recognized the potential value of the dog's aggressive instincts and shaped them—through selective breeding and training—into useful "working" attributes. People channeled the dog's innate territoriality into guarding behavior that protects hearth and home. And, as people began providing for the nutritional needs of dogs, canine predatory behavior evolved into helpful hunting, herding, and vermin-elimination behaviors.

Human Folly

Inappropriate aggression, while occasionally a result of medical disorders, is more commonly caused by human mismanagement (either intentional or unwitting). When humans mismanage their dogs, once-valuable behavior can deteriorate into aggression that (although "reasonable" from the dog's point of view) may threaten public safety.

It's not surprising that aggression is the number-one reason people bring dogs to animal behaviorists or veterinary behavior clinics for advice and treatment. The most common patients: unneutered male dogs between the ages of one and three—the time period when dogs reach sexual and social maturity.

Categorizing Aggression

Behaviorists have developed various classification schemes for canine aggression, according to the circumstances in which the behavior occurs. Recognizing these categories may help in determining a treatment for problem behavior, but more than one categorical type may apply to an individual dog.

■ Dominance Aggression
Motivation: Need to find its place in the pack hierarchy.
Target: Usually a family member, another dog in the household, or another intact male dog.

■ Fear Aggression

Motivation: Fear of an actual or perceived threat.
Target: Usually a nonfamiliar person, animal, or situation.

■ Territorial/Protective Aggression

Motivation: Perceived threat to home or pack.
Target: Usually an "alien" person or animal.

■ Pain Aggression

Motivation: Response to sickness or injury.
Target: Nearest human or animal.

■ Maternal Aggression

Motivation: Threat to young.
Target: Anyone or anything in close proximity to puppies.

■ Predatory Aggression

Motivation: Sustenance.
Target: Usually smaller animals, but sometimes infants.

■ Seizure-Related Aggression

Cause: Seizure-like brain disorders.
Target: Just about anything—animate or inanimate.

Preventing Problem Aggression

As with most canine behaviors, the best cure for problem aggression is prevention. When selecting a dog, for example, choose one that matches your expectations and lifestyle. If you are thinking about purchasing or adopting a certain type of dog, first study the breed and talk to breed owners. Remember that working and herding dogs are more likely to show aggression than others. "Such breeds are probably not good 'starter dogs' for novice owners," says Dr. Nicholas Dodman. Similar care in choosing a breeder and in selecting, socializing, and training a puppy will help you avoid aggression-related problems and improve the odds of a long-term, mutually rewarding relationship with your dog.

In addition to having an innate biological potential for aggression, dogs can also learn to be (or not be) aggressive. Lessons in aggression begin in puppyhood when youngsters learn to inhibit aggression during play with littermates. If they bite too hard, their playmates yelp, putting an end to the game. (Puppies separated from their littermates too early, however, don't learn this rule and may become problem biters.)

Sometimes people intervene in the learning process and either purposefully or inadvertently teach their dogs the opposite lesson: to be too aggressive. "People who encourage or reward their dogs for aggressive behavior are reinforcing the message that intimidation works," explains Dr. Dodman. (Something as "innocent" as permitting a puppy to chew on your fingers can lead to problems later.)

Treating Aggression Problems

It's up to owners to notice when their dogs cross the line into inappropriate aggression. At the first sign of unwanted or inappropriate aggressive behavior in your dog, seek help from a qualified animal behaviorist or a veterinarian who specializes in dog behavior. Early intervention gives your dog the best chance of changing its behavior and gives you the guidance you need to avoid reinforcing unwanted behavior.

Treatment for aggression falls into three basic categories: **training, pharmacological/surgical intervention, and avoiding provocative situations**. The right approach (or combination of approaches) depends on the individual dog and its underlying motivation .

■ Training

Dominance aggression is the most common form of aggression for which owners seek help. While these aggressive responses can be unsettling, dominant dogs are simply trying to ascend to the leadership of the family pack They often respond to firm (not harsh) obedience training followed by a behavior-modification program. "Obedience training helps you establish leadership by setting ground rules and rewarding compliance," says Dr. Dodman. Many dominant-aggressive dogs also settle down in response to a consistent "no free lunch" policy where the dog receives positive attention and rewards only after it obeys a command such as "sit" or "down."

If your dog's aggression arises from fear and/or territoriality, you may be able to desensitize it through gradual exposure to the particular objects or situations that elicit such be-

havior. Simultaneously, such dogs can be counterconditioned to associate what was once a trigger for aggression with a pleasurable experience—such as treats.

■ Surgery

Although the precise biological connections between hormones and
behavior have not yet been established, it's clear that hormones influence some forms of aggression. If your intact male dog is constantly
scrapping with other males, it may help to neuter the dog (the younger
the better) to eliminate the hormone testosterone. Similarly, hormone-
mediated maternal aggression, which sometimes accompanies false
pregnancy (pseudocyesis), can be resolved by spaying.

■ Pharmacological Aids

Pharmacological intervention can assist some aggressive dogs that
do not respond readily to behavioral approaches alone. (Such medication should be used only under the supervision of a veterinarian. Note also that the U.S. Food and Drug Administration has not
formally approved for use in dogs some drugs prescribed for aggression.)

Because aggression is a complex, coordinated response mediated
in various regions of the brain, scientists have only recently developed highly selective drugs that influence aggression without affecting other brain-mediated functions. Fluoxetine, commonly
known as Prozac™, is one such drug. It interacts with a specific re-
ceptor molecule on certain brain cell membranes to delay the reab-
sorption of one chemical, serotonin. Fluoxetine can help subdue a
dog's overbearing dominance drive Fear aggression also frequently responds to fluoxetine's anxiety-reducing properties and to beta
blockers such as propranolol, which calm the dog physiologically,
thereby increasing its ability to learn from behavior-modification
techniques. And dogs exhibiting seizure-related aggression sometimes get relief from the anticonvulsant phenobarbital .

■ Avoidance

With some aggression, it's best to simply avoid situations that set
off the behavior. For example, with maternal aggression, restrict the
number of visitors who approach the whelping box to see the new
puppies. (Maternal aggression fades as the pups mature, and it's a
good idea to expose young puppies to limited and gentle human
handling as soon as mom is ready to receive visitors.)

Dogs in pain sometimes lash out at the nearest person, even if
that person is a Good Samaritan with the best of intentions. If

you're involved in an emergency with a dog in pain, muzzle the dog (unless doing so would jeopardize its condition) before getting veterinary help. Regular veterinary checkups and extra TLC can help make elderly dogs suffering pain from chronic conditions (such as arthritis) more comfortable and reduce the chances of pain-related aggression.

Behaviorists debate whether predation, a deeply rooted, intrinsically rewarding instinctive behavior, is a form of aggression per se. (Predatory behavior in dogs does not seem to involve the mood and physiological changes associated with the "emotional" forms of aggression.)

The most effective "treatment" is to avoid situations where the instinct kicks in. For example, keep dogs that are prone to problem predatory behavior away from smaller animals.

The Paradox of Play Aggression

Playing with your dog is supposed to be a time for laughter and light-hearted antics. But play is also important to a young dog's social development. Games such as chasing and wrestling give puppies the chance to establish a position in the pack hierarchy of the litter. But be aware that "Play can escalate into aggression," warns Dr. Jean DeNapoli, a resident at the Behavior Clinic at Tufts University School of Veterinary Medicine.

Because play and aggression seem to be opposite emotions, owners are often stunned when a playing dog suddenly becomes aggressive. In fact, play and aggression are closely related. A puppy that's learned to dominate its littermates during play may transfer that bossy attitude to its future canine or human playmates—particularly while roughhousing.

Even human athletes—especially those who play contact sports—sometimes end up fighting. That's why most sports have rules limiting physical contact, referees to enforce the rules, and penalties for breaking the rules. Likewise, you can avoid canine play aggression by establishing a few simple rules and assessing "penalties" for transgressions.

Play aggression sometimes crops up when young pups play, but it usually doesn't become a problem until puberty. As with humans, play aggression occurs more frequently in male dogs than in females, perhaps due to the male sex hormone testosterone.

Unfortunately, children are often the first to confront canine play aggression because of their small size, their tendency to "get physical," and their squeaky voices that remind dogs of prey animals.

Frequently, people miss the early warning signs of play aggression because they look and sound like playful exuberance. Here are some signals that your dog may be taking play time too seriously:

■ Biting or Nipping

Watch out for the dog that bites down hard on your hand or arm or nips at you when you run.

■ Snatching or Guarding Toys

Be wary of a dog that growls if its toys are taken away or snatches them possessively when you approach.

■ Refusal to Let Go

Dogs that won't relinquish their grip on a play object or lunge to grab it again if you force them to let go are moving toward play aggression.

■ Growling, or a Change in Vocal Tone

Some dogs are naturally vociferous while playing. But an experienced listener can differentiate between aggressive sounds and harmless, playful vocalizations.

If you see or hear any signs of aggression, immediately stop the game. You effectively penalize your dog by depriving it of its favorite playmate—you. Remember, also, that repeated episodes of play aggression (or aggression in other situations) may be evidence of a serious behavior problem that warrants the attention of a qualified animal behaviorist.

Playing with your dog is tons of fun, educational and healthy for you and your dog, and a great way to strengthen your bond. But recognize the signs of incipient play aggression and teach your dog basic-obedience commands. That way, you and your canine friend can continue to have fun playing by the rules.

Preventing Play Aggression

■ Make sure your dog recognizes people as leaders, not littermates.

■ Establish leadership through positively reinforced basic-obedience training.

■ Teach your dog simple commands like "come" and "down" so

you can maintain control over all your interactions with your dog.
■ Avoid games that involve direct physical contact, such as tug-of-war and wrestling.

When Playing with Your Dog

■ Periodically assert control by stopping the game and commanding your dog into a sit-stay.

■ If your game involves a play object like a ball, tell your dog to "give" or "drop it." Stop the game and walk away if your dog refuses to comply.

■ Be alert for signs that your dog is "testing" family members, particularly children.

If Nothing Works

Sometimes owners and professionals cannot bring canine aggression under sufficient control to ensure the safety of the family, the dog, or the neighborhood. In such cases, the choices are limited. Although a very aggressive dog might respond positively to a "change of scene" in another home, it is dishonest and dangerous to place such a dog up for adoption without fully disclosing its behavior problems. On the other hand, local and national breed-rescue organizations do an excellent job placing difficult dogs with carefully screened owners who can love them and safely manage their behavior. Another option—humane euthanasia—may be the last resort in rare cases where a dog's aggression stems from incurable disease or where the behavior is so intractable that it doesn't respond to repeated attempts at treatment.

While aggression is just one aspect of a dog's behavioral repertoire, it can be the most problematic. Because canine aggression is often significantly influenced by human deeds (or misdeeds), all owners need to understand their dog's aggressive behavior and (if necessary) intervene in a timely manner to control it. ❧

28

Why Dogs Bite—
How to Prevent It

Some dogs bite because they're physically ill;
others accidentally, in play. It's important to examine
closely the circumstances surrounding the bite.

Like their human counterparts, some dogs occasionally forget their manners and lash out. Rather than using words, they may bite—a most undesirable canine behavior from our viewpoint but a natural response from a dog's. "Most dog bites occur for a reason," says Dr. Linda Aronson, a veterinary behavioral consultant in Lexington, Massachusetts. "Any dog is capable of biting given the right circumstances."

A recent study published in the *Journal of the American Medical Association* reports there are 4.5 million dog bites each year, far more than previously estimated. Because dog bites can cause physical and emotional pain, preventing them is an owner's civic and moral responsibility.

Medical Reasons

Some dogs bite because they're physically ill. "If an easygoing dog suddenly starts biting people, you've got to suspect medical causes," says Dr. Aronson. Hypothyroidism and lead poisoning can cause nervous-system abnormalities that lead to biting, and a dog having an epileptic seizure may bite unawares. Remember, too, that a dog in pain may reflexively bite anyone who attempts to touch it—even its owner. (Numerous conditions—ranging from ear infections to traumatic injuries and cancer—cause dogs pain.)

Contextual Clues

If you and your veterinarian rule out medical causes, closely examine the circumstances surrounding the bite—and the dog's perception of the situation. According to Dennis Fetko, Ph.D., an applied animal behaviorist in San Diego, California, most bites are triggered by what dogs perceive as provocation from people.

It's easy to understand why dogs that are harshly disciplined might bite. In confrontational situations, biting is driven by fear (self-defense) or dominance aggression (a dominant dog's belligerent reaction to threats to its top-dog status). And some very dominant dogs bite in response to a gentle pat on the head, which these dogs perceive as an irksome challenge to their dominance.

Exhilarated by spirited play, a dog may bite accidentally or as an expression of play aggression. Without the means to escape, a dog that is cornered or tied up may bite an approaching stranger out of fear. When a dog bites a passing bicyclist or jogger, it's usually because of predatory instincts or fear, activated when the "intruder" rapidly approaches the dog's security zone.

Fur Is Thicker than Skin

The type and location of a bite may help you determine the biter's intentions. Often preceded by growling, snarling, and other body-language clues that people sometimes overlook, a quick, snapping bite is usually intended to warn a person to "back off" rather than to inflict bodily harm. Dogs often nip each other to establish similar boundaries. But fur is thicker than skin, so the same nip that's harmless when applied to a fellow canine may cause a wound when applied to the human body. And because dogs usually bite what is closest to their vantage point, children and adults who kneel or bend over are often bitten on the face. Thankfully, it's unusual for dogs to bite people as hard as they can. In the rare case where a dog really wants to hurt someone, it will bite

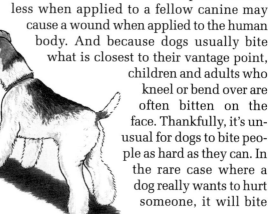

multiple times and fasten onto and shake a body part—especially the abdomen or neck. Dominant dogs tend to make frontal assaults, while fear-based and predatory strikes usually come from behind.

Kids and Dogs

Public-health records show that children are the most common targets of dog bites. And because of their shorter stature, kids are twice as likely as adults to be bitten on the face, head, or neck. Consequently, always supervise interactions between your dog and children—particularly infants and toddlers who are poorly equipped to protect themselves. And never leave a dog that has shown aggressive tendencies alone with any child.

While children that tease or harass dogs are sometimes bitten, so too are youngsters with loving intentions. "It's important to keep kids calm in the presence of dogs," notes Dennis Fetko, Ph.D., an applied animal behaviorist in San Diego, California. When an excited, squealing child rushes up to a dog to pet it, the intense stimulation can trigger a chase or defensive response that could lead to a nip. Therefore, teach children never to run, yell, poke, or pull at a dog and never to interrupt a dog that is eating, eliminating, or sleeping. Also, show children how to pet a dog from below the pooch's head. "Most kids pet from the top down, and they do it quickly, which violates the dog's concept of secure personal space," explains Dr. Fetko.

Finally, dogs that are carefully socialized with children are less likely to bite youngsters—and more likely to develop the unique devotion characteristic of most dog-children relationships.

Plotting Prevention

■ Selection

Bite prevention begins with responsible breeding to root out hereditary predispositions toward aggression. Before procuring a puppy, "interview" at least one of its parents. People-friendly progenitors usually have even-tempered offspring.

■ Socialization

Proper socialization is equally important. Affectionate handling by many different types of people teaches a puppy to associate humans with pleasure.

■ Training

You can also reduce the risk of biting through appropriate training. Positive reinforcement (praise, petting, playing, and food treats) helps create a learning environment that's not conducive to biting. "Grabby" dogs, however, sometimes bite the hand that treats them, so play or praise may be safer reinforcements. Conversely, harsh punishment can encourage biting—especially in dominant or fearful dogs.

If your dog becomes too nippy when playing, discourage the behavior by abruptly ending the play session. You can prevent accidental play bites by keeping canine excitement in check. "For example, make your dog sit and drop the toy before you throw it again," advises Dr. Aronson. And unless you're trying to build self-confidence in a shy, nonaggressive dog, avoid wrestling and tug-of-war games, which may incite competitive struggles that your dog settles with his teeth.

Timely Treatment

Take all biting incidents seriously, and seek a remedy quickly. Because retraining a dog that bites can be dangerous, we highly recommend competent, humane professional assistance to help you understand why your dog bit and what you should do about it.

Behavior modification is the first-line treatment for biters. Dogs that bite out of fear or territoriality often improve after desensitization—a process that gradually teaches the dog to be less reactive to bite-provoking stimuli. A "no free lunch" approach where a dog must earn everything it wants, including food and attention, often helps reform dogs that bite out of dominance-related aggression. Along with behavior modification, some biters also benefit from medication such as fluoxetine (Prozac), which increases the brain's level of the neurotransmitter serotonin. Increased daily exercise also may help.

Unfortunately, there are a few dogs whose behavior is so uncontrollable that euthanasia is the most appropriate option. But in most cases, biting is an explainable and treatable offense, not one that should automatically sentence a dog to death. ❖

29

Chew on This!

*Normal chewing cleans your dog's
teeth, massages its gums, and exercises its jaws.
But dog owners need to channel this instinct.*

Like their lupine predecessors, dogs boast impressive chewing apparatus—powerful jaws and 42 permanent teeth designed to grip, gnaw, crush, and tear. While this mouthful of equipment helped Bowser's ancestors survive, he hardly ever needs to capture and shred his food. Yet, driven by instinct, dogs still need to chew, and if owners don't channel this instinct, it can wreak havoc with a dog's health—and the household furnishings.

"C-H-E-W" Spells Pain Relief

Chewing is part of normal jaw and tooth development. Young puppies chew largely to relieve the discomfort associated with tooth eruption (teething). And the temporary comfort that chewing provides encourages further chewing.

Although pups tend to chew indiscriminately, you can teach them what's appropriate and safe to chew. Before you bring your new pup home, procure several safe and tooth-healthy chew toys, such as resilient Gumabones®. Also, comb your dog's new habitat and remove as many household chewables as possible.

"Every time your pup chews something you don't want it chewing, firmly say 'out' or 'leave it'—then remove the object and replace it with an acceptable chew toy," recommends Dr. Nicholas

Dodman, director of the Behavior Clinic at Tufts University School of Veterinary Medicine. You can also steer your pup in the right direction if you add flavoring to its "chewies" or use them as toys during play sessions.

To relieve teething pain that triggers chewing, "freeze a rolled-up wet washcloth and give it to your pup to chew on," suggests Dr. Laura LeVan, clinical assistant professor at Tufts University School of Veterinary Medicine. But retrieve the washcloth before it thaws; otherwise, your dog might think similar accessories—like hand towels—are fair game for chewing.

When you can't directly supervise your puppy's chewing escapades, consider confining it to a warm, comfortable crate. But make sure you first accustom the pup to its "den" by feeding and playing with it inside the crate. If your pup doesn't shred and eat chew toys, leave a chew toy in the crate. Don't try this with a zealous chomper, however.

Chewing Away Stress

Some adult dogs chew to relieve emotional stress—especially stress caused by separation anxiety or lack of environmental stimulation—what we call boredom Stress-related chewing almost always occurs when the owner's not present, but even a relaxed dog may chew "when the cat's away" if it has previously been punished for chewing.

To resolve chewing caused by separation anxiety, you may have to try several techniques. None, however, involve punishment, which only makes matters worse. First, take the emotion out of your comings and goings by completely ignoring your dog for 15 minutes before leaving and after returning. "Trick" your dog into thinking you're on your way out by grabbing your keys, your coat, and so on—and then sit quietly in a chair. But focus most of your effort on graduated departures. Leave your dog alone for short, then gradually increasing, periods of time. Increase your "stay away" time only when your dog seems OK with the last separation period.

Some dogs that chew due to separation anxiety go berserk when crated, so confinement may not be a viable option. Some dogs benefit from antianxiety medication, but a few may not adapt to solitude under any circumstances. Such pooches may require a full-time pet sitter or a reputable "doggie day care" facility.

If boredom fuels your dog's destructive chewing, enliven its "home alone" environment. The simplest form of environmental enrichment is 30 to 60 minutes of daily aerobic exercise. Be consistent with exercise, though, because dogs may turn to destructive chewing when they exercise only sporadically.

WELL-EXERCISED DOGS ARE TOO

TUCKERED OUT TO ENGAGE IN

DESTRUCTIVE CHEWING!

Preventing Problem Chewing

You can try to divert your dog from problem chewing by carefully selecting toys and avoiding certain types of games. Never give your dog old shoes, socks, or clothing as chew toys. As savvy as dogs are, they can't tell a worn pair of slippers from brand-new dress shoes. For similar reasons, steer clear of toys that resemble household items, like shoe-shaped rawhide chews. And avoid overindulging your dog with too many toys. "A dog with 23 toys may get the idea that anything is OK to chew on," cautions Dr. Dennis Fetko, Ph.D., a San Diego-based applied animal behaviorist. Tug-of-war games also may encourage excessive chewing (not to mention aggression).

You can also minimize the risk of problem chewing by obedience training and socializing your dog with people and other dogs so it develops confidence and independence. Additionally, refrain from any behavior your dog might construe as a reward for chewing. For example, don't replace an inappropriate chewable with a food treat. "Although you're redirecting the dog to an acceptable object, the dog thinks it's getting a tasty reward for chewing the chair," says Dr. Fetko.

Although most canine chewing problems involve too much chewing, occasionally a dog will chew less than usual. "Dogs with painful teeth or gums often chew slowly or on one side of their mouth," explains Dr. LeVan. "Take note of your dog's normal chewing habits, and contact your veterinarian if you see any changes one way or another." No matter how carefully you "chew proof" your home, your dog may still manage to find unsafe or inappropriate chewables. If you can't eliminate such chew objects from your household, you can at least try to make them aversive.

The handiest approach is to use one of several commercial sprays or ointments that impart a bad taste to household objects. But hot chili sauce, alum (a bitter-tasting, saltlike substance that you can dissolve and "paint" on surfaces), and Vicks® VapoRub® are "home-made" potions you can also use to deter chewers that seem "immune" to commercial products.

Taste aversion has two advantages: it works even when you're absent, and your dog associates the unpleasantness with the target object—not with you. But don't use this technique if your dog chews to relieve anxiety. With anxiety-based chewing, even such a mild punishment may raise anxiety levels and worsen bad behavior. ♣

30

Medicating Misbehavior

*Modern psychoactive drugs are part of the arsenal
used by veterinarians today to treat
certain types of unmanageable canine behavior.*

It's unlikely you'll ever be able to give your dog a "magic pill" to permanently cure troublesome behavior. But medication can sometimes beneficially influence canine behavior. Today, veterinarians are beginning to prescribe psychoactive (mind-affecting) drugs to help treat dogs with hard-to-manage behavior problems, including fears and phobias, certain types of aggression, and compulsive behavior.

However, with veterinary guidance, a determined and patient owner can usually solve most garden-variety behavior problems (such as jumping on people) without resorting to medication. Still, medication can be a helpful ally when you're dealing with implacable problems that more traditional approaches have failed to correct—or problems so serious that they threaten the well-being of your dog—or you.

Some veterinarians also prescribe medication as a "pharmacological shoehorn" to help a canine patient become more emotionally receptive to behavior modification. (Behavior modification trains a dog to respond more appropriately to whatever prompts misbehavior.) Says Dr. Barbara Simpson of the Veterinary Behavior Clinic in Southern Pines, North Carolina, "Behavioral therapy in dogs is often most successful when it combines behavior modification with pharmacology." Adds Dr. Nicholas Dodman, "The behavior cases that respond to nothing but medication are few and far between."

Behavior and Brain Chemistry

At its most basic level, your dog's behavior is mediated by electrical and chemical communication between nerve cells (neurons). Electrical impulses traveling down one nerve cell cause the release of chemical neurotransmitters. These chemicals cross the tiny gap between the cells and stimulate neighboring neurons to "fire," thus transmitting a signal.

Although researchers haven't yet pinpointed the neurons responsible for behavior, levels of certain neurotransmitters in the brain—most notably catecholamines, serotonin, and gamma-aminobutyric acid (GABA)—seem to affect canine behavior. Catecholamines such as dopamine help regulate motor activity. Serotonin modulates the effects of other neurotransmitters and may influence dominance-related behavior in dogs. GABA is an inhibitory neurotransmitter that helps "cool the jets" during overactive emotional states.

The newest drugs veterinarians are using in canine behavioral therapy either boost or inhibit the effects of specific neurotransmitters. They usually do not have sedative effects—unlike most of the older-generation drugs, such as tranquilizers. Veterinarians prefer nonsedating drugs because drowsy dogs can't learn well during behavior-modification exercises.

Canine Candidates

Before prescribing behavior-modifying medication, the veterinarian will give your dog a complete physical exam to rule out any underlying physical cause of the behavior. He /she will also ask specific questions about your dog's behavior. Try to provide precise answers to help the practitioner arrive at a diagnosis. If your dog has no underlying medical condition, the veterinarian will probably recommend specific behavior-modification techniques that will gradually teach your dog to cope with the people, places, or things that incite its inappropriate behavior. The veterinarian may also recommend certain environmental changes, such as increased exercise.

If medication seems to be the way to go, your practitioner will review your dog's medical history and may perform some laboratory tests to home in on the safest drug for the situation. To help you monitor your dog's progress, your veterinarian will describe how the medication is likely to alter your dog's behavior and what possible side effects it may have. Veterinarians are especially cautious about prescribing psychoactive medication for elderly dogs or patients with preexisting medical ailments. Also, never give your dog medication without your veterinarian's counsel!

Veterinarians report that the newer psychoactive medications cause few noticeable side effects in our canine companions. However, your veterinarian may ask you to sign a consent form before prescribing psychoactive medication. That's because most drugs used in canine behavioral therapy are presently approved for use only in people by the U.S. Food and Drug Administration, although several clinical trials involving dogs are in progress.

Rx Roster

■ Aggression

The most problematic behavior in dogs is aggression. Most such cases stem from dominance-related behavior—when one dog tries to assume "top dog" status over another dog or person. Behavior-modification programs often succeed in reducing aggression, but medication may yield even more improvement.

In at least one study, dogs with severe dominance-related aggression had lower brain levels of serotonin compared to nonaggressive dogs. So, drugs that increase serotonin levels, such as fluoxetine (commonly known as Prozac®), may help control dominance-related aggression.

■ Phobic Fidos

Many canine behavior problems involve fear and anxiety—such as fear of loud noises (particularly thunder) and anxiety when a dog is left alone (separation anxiety). Dogs suffering from such disorders may become so stressed that they urinate, defecate, or become destructive. Medication can sometimes accelerate the painstaking process of desensitizing a dog to a feared stimulus and help reduce anxiety more quickly.

For anxiety and fears, veterinarians often prescribe a tricyclic antidepressant such as amitriptyline (commonly known as Elavil®) or a serotonin-reuptake inhibitor such as fluoxetine. In the brain, these drugs increase serotonin levels by preventing released serotonin from being reabsorbed.

Buspirone is another serotonin booster that seems to work best in dogs suffering from "social" anxiety—where, for example, changes in the "family pack" lead to indoor urine marking. Benzodiazepines (including diazepam or Valium®) mimic the calming effects of the body's naturally inhibitory neurotransmitter gamma-aminobutyric acid. Unfortunately, benzodiazepines have a short period of effectiveness, result in sedation, and sometimes cause physical dependence.

■ Compulsive Canines

Stereotypies (purposeless and potentially harmful repetition of specific behaviors) are notoriously difficult to treat with behavior-modification techniques alone. Some scientists think excessive amounts of the chemical dopamine may contribute to certain motion-oriented stereotypies such as tail chasing. Consequently, dopamine blockers in combination with serotonin-enhancing drugs often work well on these repetitive behaviors.

Pups on Prozac

During a recent edition of NBC's "TV Nation," millions of viewers saw Willy the bull terrier miraculously overcome his lifelong infatuation with a log, following treatment with Prozac. The next day, veterinarians and veterinary schools from coast to coast fielded calls from people demanding Prozac for their dogs.

Physicians frequently prescribe Prozac (the trade name for fluoxetine) to treat depression in people. Clinical studies investigating the effectiveness of Prozac (and similar compounds) in dogs are still under way. But anecdotal evidence suggests that these drugs can help solve certain canine behavior problems—especially in cases where traditional behavior modification has failed to get results.

"However," cautions Dr. Nicholas Dodman, director of the Behavior Clinic at Tufts University School of Veterinary Medicine, "Prozac is not a panacea. It must be administered properly, starting with a low dose and gradually building up to an effective dose for the particular dog."

Prozac and several similar drugs act on specific neurons (nerve cells) that release the chemical serotonin into the gap (synapse) between neurons. In people, low serotonin levels are associated with depression; high serotonin levels correlate to anxiety. Prozac prevents serotonin-producing neurons from reabsorbing the chemical after its release, which results in increased serotonin levels in the synapse. Consequently, Prozac and related compounds are called selective serotonin reuptake inhibitors (SSRIs).

Veterinarians are interested in the apparent potential of SSRIs to help modify dominance-related aggression and compulsive behavior in dogs. The SSRIs target a specific neurochemical culprit without sedating the patient and with fewer side effects than most other behavior-altering drugs. (Veterinarians should not administer SSRIs to dogs with histories of seizures. But relatively minor side effects, such as anxiety or hyperactivity, can be addressed by reducing the dosage.)

Veterinarians have used Prozac as an adjunct in certain difficult dominance-aggression cases. "In dogs," says Dr. Dodman, "high and somewhat fluctuating levels of serotonin are characteristic of dominance. If owners of dominant-aggressive dogs aren't making satisfactory progress with behavior modification, SSRIs might be indicated. Early evidence indicates that these drugs help make such dogs more composed."

The drugs have also proven invaluable in treating some compulsively repetitive behavior in dogs, such as lick granuloma (instinctive grooming behavior gone awry) and obsessive "shadow chasing." The jury is still out, however, on whether SSRIs are effective in treating fear and anxiety conditions (such as noise phobias and separation anxiety).

Although SSRIs may appear to be "wonder drugs" in and of themselves, they should be used as part of a treatment program. Solving most canine behavior problems depends on accurate diagnosis; behavior modification with owner support and commitment; and adjustments in diet, environment, and exercise routines. It is never quite as simple as "just popping a pill."

Drug Drawbacks

Despite advances in pharmacology, "individual dogs respond differently to behavior-modifying medications, so there is no guarantee that these drugs will work in all cases," cautions Dr. Dodman. Consequently, veterinarians often have to change the type of drug and/or adjust the dosage before the owner sees significant improvement.

Another potential disadvantage is that many psychoactive drugs take as long as 4 to 8 weeks to reach levels that will alter behavior. Cost is another drawback. While many animals can be weaned off medication gradually, some require a long-term course of medication, which can be costly. (Dosage is usually weight-dependent, so treating a mastiff will probably cost significantly more than treating a Chihuahua.)

Remember that you and your veterinarian can treat many behavior problems without pharmacological aids. When medication is indicated, though, it's part of an overall treatment program, not a stand-alone miracle cure. While medication helps with some resistant behavior, there's no substitute for consistent and gentle behavior-modification training for most misbehaving dogs. ❧

31

A Calming TTouch

The Tellington TTouch is an alternative approach to dealing with phobias, working wonders with fear-based and/or habitual response patterns.

It's five a.m. You're suddenly awakened by a sound. After a moment you roll over and go back to sleep, realizing it's Tuesday and thinking dark thoughts about garbage trucks. Your noise-phobic dog, however, may not only think the sky is falling, but also that it's his responsibility to make sure that everyone in the world knows about it. So much for sleep.

When the average dog hears a loud or unusual noise, as long as no one around him panics or acts strangely, he'll generally figure out that there is nothing to worry about. But noise-phobic dogs don't seem to notice that the earth just keeps turning, noise or no noise. And, for many of these dogs, noises can elicit problem behavior of varying natures: territorial, fear-based, obsessive/habitual, to name a few.

This need not be a permanent condition. Training a dog can change a dog's response to a noisy event. But training alone does not always relieve the underlying fear-based stress caused by the noise phobia in the first place, and, may in fact, contribute to its continuation. Instead, the dog may change the focus of his stress to another sound or sense; some begin exhibiting other problem behavior, such as destructive chewing or obsessive licking.

This is where Tellington TTouch can make a difference. While TTouch works to help every animal become better balanced and more consciously responsive to itself and its environment, it is with the fear-based and/or habitual response patterns that TTouch can truly work wonders.

Left, Sabra's left hand rests on Honey's shoulder. With her right hand, she gently holds Honey's right ear. Right, as Honey relaxes, Sabra uses the Ear Slide with both hands.

Tellington TTouch

TTouch body work and learning exercises affect the nervous system, interrupting habitual patterns and giving dogs the opportunity to discover and experience their own ability to respond to challenging situations in new and different ways – to think, not just react.

Improving the communication between the body and the mind promotes physical, mental, and emotional balance. Given a choice, a balanced dog will release old patterns and choose less stressful, more rewarding, more efficient patterns – ones that, with your guidance, will be mutually beneficial (aahhh, blessed sleep!).

For some dogs, the change can be instant. One Great Dane used to be so terrified of thunder that she would pull the couch away from the wall and hide behind it when a storm hit, damaging both the wall and the couch in the process. She had one session of TTouch (when there was no thunder), and during the next storm was found lying *on* the couch, fast asleep. Now, that's letting go of baggage!

On the other hand, a nervous Border Collie with incredibly sensitive hearing might need TTouch on a regular basis to help him maintain his balance, and his family might always have to be mindful of the level of sound in their home and surroundings to reduce the stress, and possibly, the pain of excessive noise. (Those fine-tuned ears are a benefit in the far hills of Scotland, but a real detriment in a city that echoes with noise around the clock.)

The following TTouch exercises can be particularly helpful with noise-related issues. Start when you and your dog are calm, so he develops trust in your touch and its results. From your dog's perspective, it feels good, it's relaxing, and it enhances communication between you. This will create memories (both mental and physical) that will be useful when he's not so calm.

Remember that TTouch works on the nervous system and a little can go a long way. Your dog needs time to process the new information, so shorter sessions of two to 10 minutes, twice a day, will be more effective than longer, more intense ones.

Ear Slides

This TTouch can help balance the entire body. Most dogs like having their ears touched, so it's usually a safe place to start. Sit beside or behind your dog with one hand gently resting on his shoulder or supporting his chin. Curl the fingers of your other hand softly and place your thumb behind and at the base of the ear with your curled

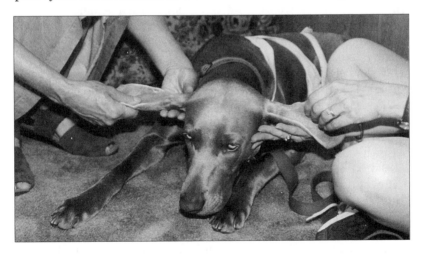

Two people perform Ear Slides on this Weimaraner at the same time. Each person is using both hands: one to support the base of the ear while the other applies the sliding pressure. This two-handed technique works well on long- or heavy-eared dogs.

fingers in front of the ear, holding gently. Slide your hand from the base of the ear to the tip and off, in the natural direction of the dog's ear. Cover the entire ear with repeated slides, keeping your hand and body relaxed and breathing naturally.

For cropped or very small ears, use just your thumb and index finger; for large, heavy ears, use one hand to support the base of the ear while your other hand does the slides. You can also rotate the entire ear in both directions holding the base as above.

Watch your dog's responses and experiment with different positions, pressures, and speeds to discover what he really likes best. For many dogs this is a great pleasure. But if he seems to really hate it, there might be a physical reason for the discomfort, so you might want to have his ears checked to eliminate this possibility.

If your dog is responding to the sound of a *perceived* threat, generally he will not want his ears touched at that time – he needs all of his senses undisturbed so that he can evaluate the potential threat. If you can anticipate when a disturbing noise is about to occur (such as sirens that go off every Saturday at noon), do some ear slides before and after and apply the Body Wrap.

The Body Wrap

The body wrap is a wonderful tool for dogs with a tendency to "lose it" when it's noisy or those unsure and fearful in their response to noise. The results can be amazing. The body wrap helps give the dog a better sense of his physical self; and connects all his parts into a whole for better balance and self-awareness. Like a hug, it can be comforting and supportive, and help him be "present"in the moment.

Depending on the size of your dog, use one or two Ace bandages, the regular stretchy ones. If you use two, you can sew or knot them together. Wrap the bandages in a figure eight around the dog's chest, across his back, under his tail, and then safety pin (diaper pins work best) or knot the ends together.

If your dog is very sensitive about his rear end (a sure sign that he could really use a body wrap), start with a half-wrap. With the middle of the wrap across his chest, cross over his shoulders, cross under the belly and back up, and pin or knot everything so that neither the pin nor the knot is directly on his spine. The tension should be even everywhere – a bit like underwear elastic. Check to make sure no hairs are caught in an uncomfortable position.

It's perfectly safe to leave the wrap on the dog for up to a couple of hours, as long as he is under constant supervision. Encourage him

Rupert models a basic Figure Eight body wrap. A single Ace bandage has been wrapped around his chest, crossing over his back, and wrapping around his rear end, under his tail. The ends of the bandage are knotted or safety-pinned together.

Once the wrap is on, run your hands under the bandage and adjust the tension so that it is even all the way around. The goal is to give the dog a "hugged" sensation, increasing his awareness of his entire body as he stands, sits, lies down, or n moves about.

to move about to enhance the "feel" of his connectedness; walking up and down stairs with the wrap on is particularly helpful. If you're without a body wrap and he really needs one, just drape a towel or jacket over him.

Experiment with the wraps and slides. Each dog is unique. The wonderful thing about TTouch is that no matter what the breed, temperament, or issue, it can enhance the trust and communication between you. This makes problem-solving both possible and probable. And you'll both sleep well. ❧

Contacts & Resources

Organizations

■ Tufts University School of Veterinary Medicine, 200 Westboro Road, North Grafton, MA 01536; (508) 839-5395

■ American Holistic Veterinary Medical Association (AHVMA), 2214 Old Emmorton Road, Bel Air, MD 21015. (410) 569-0795; www.altvetmed.com.

■ Academy of Veterinary Homeopathy (AVH), 751 NE 168th Street, North Miami, FL 33162. (305) 652-1590. Referrals. www.theavh.org

■ International Veterinary Acupuncture Society (IVAS), PO Box 1478, Longmont, CO 80502. (303) 682-1167.

■ The American Veterinary Chiropractic Association directory, 623 Main Street, Hillsdale, IL 61257; (309) 658-2920.

Phobias/Noise

Storm recordings: K-9 Communications, Glenview, IL; (847) 729-0490; and Syntonic Research, Inc., Austin, TX (800) 659-4345.

Books

■ The Dog and Cat Book Catalog, (800) 776-2665; ■ Everything in Dog Books, (800) 487-9867; Valerie Cline, Barney's Choice: ■ Source for alternative health care books for dogs and cats. 5345 rue St. Urbain, Montreal, Quebec, Canada H2T 2W8; P:(514) 279-2075; F: (514) 279-0658.

On Talking Terms With Dogs: Calming Signals, Turid Rugaas, Legacy, P.O. Box 3909, Sequim, WA 98382. (360) 683-1522; www.Legacy-By-Mail.com.

The UC Davis Book of Dogs, edited by Mordecai Siegal. 1995, HarperCollins Publishers, New York, NY. ISBN 0-06-270136-3.

Clicker Training for Obedience, Morgan Spector. ISBN 0-9624017-8-1.

Home-Prepared Dog & Cat Diets, Dr. Donald R. Strombeck. ISBN 0-8138-2149-5.

The Encyclopedia of Natural Pet Care, C.J. Puotinen. ISBN 0-87983-797-7.

"Four Paws, Five Directions: A guide to Chinese medicine for cats and dogs," Dr. Cheryl Schwartz. 406 pages,$24.95.1996, Celestial Arts, Berkeley, CA, (800) 841-2665.

Dr. Pitcairn's Complete Guide to Natural Health for Dogs & Cats, Dr. Richard Pitcairn. 1995, St. Martin's Press. 383 pages, $17. ISBN # 0-87596-243-2

The Complete Herbal Handbook for the Dog and Cat, Juliette de Bairacli Levy. 1992, Faber & Faber. 345 pages, $15. ISBN # 0-571-16115-4

The Natural Remedy Book for Dogs & Cats, Diane Stein. 1997, The Crossing Press. 331 pages, $17. ISBN # 0-89594-686-6

The Holistic Guide for a Healthy Dog, Wendy Volhard and Kerry Brown, DVM. 1995, Howell Book House. 294 pages, $27. ISBN# 0-87605-560-9

Dr. Nicholas H. Dodman: *Dogs Behaving Badly: An A-to-Z Guide to Understanding and Curing Behavioral Problems in Dogs,* 1999; *The Dog Who Loved Too Much: Tales, Treatments, and the Psychology of Dogs,* 1998; *Psychopharmacology of Animal Behavior Disorders,* 1998. Available from amazon.com.

How To Teach a New Dog Old Tricks, 192 pgs., $17.95; *Dr. Dunbar's Good Little Dog Book,* 80 pgs., $15), Dr. Ian Dunbar; James & Kenneth Publishers, Dept. 3492, 2140 Shattuck Avenue #2406, Berkeley, CA 94704; (800) 784-5531 or (510) 658-8588.

Videos

Sirius Puppy Training, 90 min., $29.95; *Training Dogs With Dunbar,* 65 min., $24.95; and *Dog Training for Children,* 83 min. $24.95; *Dog Aggression: Fighting* (60 min., $24.95) and *Dog Aggression: Biting* (90 min., $24.95). James & Kenneth Publishers, Dept. 3492, 2140 Shattuck Avenue #2406, Berkeley, CA 94704; (800) 784-5531 or (510) 658-8588. ❧

Index